Solipsism

Other Books of Interest from St. Augustine's Press

Richard A. Watson, *Descartes' Ballet*

Peter Kreeft, *Socrates' Children* (in four volumes):
Ancient, Medieval, Modern, and *Contemporary*

Peter Kreeft, *Summa Philosophica*

Gerhart Niemeyer, *The Loss and Recovery of Truth*

Stanley Rosen, *Essays in Philosophy* (in two volumes):
Ancient and *Modern*

Stanley Rosen, *Platonic Productions:*
Theme and Variations: The Gilson Lectures

Gabriel Marcel, *The Mystery of Being* (in two volumes):
I: *Reflections and Mystery* and II: *Faith and Reality*

Seth Benardete, *The Archaeology of the Soul*

Philippe Bénéton, *The Kingdom Suffereth Violence:*
The Machiavelli / Erasmus / More Correspondence

Rémi Brague, *On the God of the Christians*
(and on one or two others)

Rémi Brague, *Eccentric Culture: A Theory of Western Civilization*

Pierre Manent, *Seeing Things Politically*

Albert Camus, *Christian Metaphysics and Neoplatonism*

Christopher Bruell, *Aristotle as Teacher:*
His Introduction to a Philosophic Science

Barry Cooper, *Consciousness and Politics:*
From Analysis to Meditation in the Late Work of Eric Voegelin

Josef Pieper, *What Does "Academic" Mean?*
Two Essays on the Chances of the University Today

Emanuela Scribano, *A Reading Guide to Descartes'*
Meditations on First Philosophy

Roger Scruton, *The Meaning of Conservatism*

René Girard, *A Theater of Envy: William Shakespeare*

H.D. Gerdil, *The Anti-Emile: Reflections on the Theory and*
Practice of Education against the Principles of Rousseau

Joseph Cropsey, *On Humanity's Intensive Introspection*

Solipsism
The Ultimate Empirical Theory of Human Existence

Richard A. Watson

Professor of Philosophy Emeritus
Washington University in St. Louis
Affiliate Professor of Philosophy, University of Montana

THE SPECTER HAUNTING MODERN PHILOSOPHY IS NOT THE GHOST IN THE MACHINE: IT IS SOLIPSISM.

ST. AUGUSTINE'S PRESS
South Bend, Indiana

Manufactured in the United States of America

1 2 3 4 5 6   22 21 20 19 18 17 16

Library of Congress Cataloging in Publication Data
Watson, Richard A., 1931–
Solipsism: the ultimate empirical theory of human existence /
Richard A. Watson, Professor of Philosophy Emeritus, Washington
University in St. Louis, Affiliate Professor of Philosophy, University
of Montana. – 1 [edition].
pages cm
"The specter haunting modern philosophy is not the ghost in the
machine: it is solipsism."
Includes bibliographical references and index.
ISBN 978-1-58731-589-3 (clothbound: alk. paper) 1. Solipsism I.
Title.
BD201.W38 2014
121'.2 – dc23   2014004577

ST. AUGUSTINE'S PRESS
www.staugustine.net

TABLE OF CONTENTS

ACKNOWLEDGMENTS

For discussions and suggestions I thank Carl Craver, Alan Gabbey, Gary Hatfield, Patrick Henry, Louise Hildebolt, William Lycan, Steven Nadler, Henry Shapiro, and Douglas Walker.

EPIGRAPHS

I am, I exist, that is certain.
But how often?
Just when I think . . .
I am a real thing and really exist, but what thing?
A thing that thinks . . .
I see light, I hear noise, I feel heat . . .
But, it will be said . . .
I am dreaming . . .

René Descartes
Meditations on First Philosophy, 1641

Is it for now or for always . . .
Shine out, my sudden angel,
Break fear with breast and brow,
I take you now and for always,
For always is always now.

Philip Larkin

Solipsism of the Present Moment

Neither future nor past exists . . .
neither the future nor the past is now present.
—Saint Augustine, *Confessions* (xii, 24)

Prefatory Note
I do not profess to be a solipsist.
I simply argue that there is no refutation of solipsism.

This fact is met in the immense contemporary literature on consciousness and the mind (see notice of a small selection in the bibliography below) with almost total silence. The ontological gap between one's private conscious mind and one's public material body remains as great today as it was for Augustine and Descartes.

* * *

There are at least a hundred recent books on consciousness, the mind, and the brain. Here are a few of the most important and influential (full references in Bibliography):

Ned Block, Owen Flanagan, and Güven Güzeldere. *The Nature of Consciousness.* 1997.
David J. Chalmers. *The Conscious Mind.* 1996.
Daniel C. Dennett. *Conscioussness Explained.* 1991.
Owen Flanagan. *Consciousness Reconsidered.* 1992.
Ted Honderich. *On Consciousness.* 2004.
William G. Lycan. *Consciousness.* 1987.
William G. Lycan. *Consciousness and Experience.* 1996.
Gareth B. Matthews. *Thought's Ego in Augustine and Descartes.* 1992.

1

Colin McGinn. *The Mysterious Flame: Conscious Minds in a Material World*. 1999.
Thomas Nagel. *Mind & Cosmos: Why the Materialist Neo-Darwinian Conception of Nature is Almost Certainly False*. 2012.
John R. Searle. *Minds, Brains and Science*. 1984.
John R. Searle. *The Rediscovery of the Mind*. 1992.
John R. Searle. *The Mystery of Consciousness*. 1997.

I know of only one serious book on solipsism itself:
William Todd. *Analytical Solipsism*. 1968.

Solipsism

Solipsism is the ontological position that only one self-conscious being exists in the universe: oneself. This conclusion is the ultimate result of the Cartesian search for absolute certainty in Western philosophy. The only certain knowledge this lone consciousness has is that it knows for certain that it exists only at the moment it is aware that it is conscious, which is the present moment. This is the foundation of the metaphysics of solipsism of the present moment: that the universe consists only of one self-consciousness being, and that this solipsist exists only in the present moment.

Solipsism of the Present Moment

As developed in detail by George Santayana (see chapter below), solipsism of the present moment is based on the empirical fact that one is conscious only of one moment—the present moment. The basic problem in explicating solipsism of the present moment is how to explain how the solipsist has the mistaken sense that time is passing and that events are succeeding one another. I explain how this temporal illusion takes place after first outlining the source in Western philosophy of the doctrine of solipsism itself.

Solipsism of the present moment is the ultimate result of the empirical search for certainty—for absolutely certain knowledge—initiated by Descartes in Modern philosophy. The solipsistic position that only one conscious being exists in the universe is derived from Descartes's "*Cogito ergo sum*," traditionally translated as "I think, therefore I am," but more precisely and adequately translated as "I am thinking, and only when I am thinking, then I am existing." Descartes introduced the *Cogito* into Modern Philosophy in 1637 in his *Discourse on Method* (CMS I 127; AT VI 32), but discusses its implications in detail only in his *Meditations on First Philosophy* of 1641. In the *Meditations*, Descartes proposes the hypothesis that

> some malicious demon of the utmost power and cunning has employed all his energies in order to deceive me. I shall think that the sky, the air, the earth, colors, shapes, sounds, and all external things are merely the delusions of dreams which he has devised to ensnare my judgment. I shall consider myself as not having hands or eyes, or flesh, or blood or senses, but as falsely believing that I have all these things. (CSM II 15; AT VII 22–23)

Then he proposes the possibility that leads to solipsism:
Descartes clearly understands the solipsistic implications of the phrase "*Cogito ergo sum*"—that one is certain one exists only when

one is conscious of thinking. Descartes purports to extract himself from this solipsism with his proof for the existence of God, Whom he believes would not so deceive him. There is no indication that he ever took solipsism seriously—as a serious possibility—or even focused on its implications, but nevertheless, his raising its possibility in the *Meditations* places him as the primal source of its initiation into Modern Philosophy.

Solipsism of the present moment, as remarked above, can be seen as an extreme result of the quest for certainty initiated by Descartes. Immediate awareness of sensory experience and ideas is the only certain evidence one can have that something—or anything—exists. And all that one has immediate consciousness of are the sensations and ideas that one is aware of in the present moment—the only moment during which or at which one can be absolutely certain that one exists. Moreover, solipsism of the present moment is the only theory of the nature and content of the universe that is based on absolutely certain knowledge, i.e., one's immediate, certain knowledge of the sensations and ideas one is conscious of at the present moment. And one knows with absolute certainty that one exists as the awareness of that experience now at the present moment.

The search for absolute certainty that René Descartes set Modern philosophy on in the seventeenth century has been rejected as a dead-end or will-o-the-wisp at least since the advent of Logical Positivism in the 1930s. Positivists also generally reject solipsism both from a common-sense viewpoint and from a scientific standpoint.

That the ordinary objects of naïve realism—such as tables and chairs—and the theoretical objects of scientific realism—such as atoms and electrons—exist, is not, and cannot ever be, known with absolute certainty. This does not—and should not—bother most people, who common-sensically believe that nothing is certain. But in fact, absolute certainty is available in one's consciousness of the present moment, and the amount of absolutely certain knowledge one can have in the present moment is immense.

Has solipsism ever been taken seriously? I examine below some woefully inadequate attempted refutations of solipsism by Idealists in a separate chapter on Idealism, but with their sustaining faith in the Absolute or God, Idealists find it difficult to consider solipsism as a serious possibility. The approach to solipsism as being ridiculous, and the assumption that anyone who takes it seriously is in need of careful explication of the tenets of Idealism or (later) of Logical Positivism, does, however, support my claim in this book that, except for George Santayana, solipsism has seldom been considered to be worth taken seriously in the Western tradition, and thus until Santayana never, except by Idealists, been seriously considered even to be worth refuting.

But, the foundational fact about human knowledge and existence, as Descartes makes clear with his *Cogito ergo sum*, is that one knows for certain only that one exists in the present moment of self-consciousness—in the present moment when one is conscious of one's present sensations such as tactile feelings, odors, sounds, tastes, and visual images; of intelligible ideas or concepts such as those of mathematics, physics, chemistry, and biology; of feelings such as those of emotions, guilt, anger, of general pleasure and pain, moral and aesthetic feelings; of conscious mental states of all kinds.

It may seem to one that one existed in the past because in one's present moment of consciousness one has thoughts that appear to be memories that record thoughts one had in the past. But David Hume (whom I discuss in a separate chapter below) points out that—like all sensations and ideas—these apparent memories actually exist only in one's consciousness in the present moment, and their apparent reference to and record of past events is an illusion. Memory-ideas thus provide certain knowledge only of what one is conscious of in the present moment. The impression that memories constitute records of anything one perceived in the past is a delusion.

The presence of memory-ideas in the present moment also engenders the illusion that one is passing through time. It seems as though one's consciousness continuously proceeds through time, but in fact one is always conscious of ideas and sensations (including memories) only in the present moment.

The first major philosopher to point this out—and to worry about it—was Saint Augustine, in his *Confessions* (xii, 13–24). Augustine says that "neither future nor past exists . . . neither the future nor the past is now present" (xii, 24). Augustine did not, however, become a solipsist. He put his faith in God as the Creator of a world containing many human beings, each of whom has an independent and private mind or soul of its own.

The most difficult stumbling block to understanding the thesis of solipsism of the present moment is that this thesis implies that one's sense of time passing is an illusion. This illusion of time passing is so intense that it is very difficult to overcome. David Hume explained it by saying that at each (necessarily present) moment, one is conscious of a set of memory ideas and sensations. This set is specified as consisting of memories in that each member of the set constitutes an image of things and events that have about them the sense of having occurred sequentially farther and farther back in time. This aspect of sequentiality is the cause of the illusion that one's consciousness is passing through time. But as Augustine, Descartes, and Hume make clear, *one is never conscious except at the present moment*. One thus does not and cannot experience any actual passing of time or any actual succession of ideas and sensations. Again, the impression that time is passing—that a succession of ideas and sensations proceeds through one's consciousness—is an illusion perpetrated by one's not focusing on the fact that one is aware of ideas and sensations only in the present moment. And because the condition of being perceived—that of being an object of conscious awareness—is the essential condition of the existence of ideas and sensations—they exist only when they actually are being perceived, which is in the present moment that they are being perceived.

Memory ideas may seem (falsely) to provide knowledge of a past, but even if there were a way that they could provide reports of past experiences, there is no way of going back to that presumed past to determine or confirm that they do. But that is beside the point. In fact, from one's sensations and ideas—all of which one is aware only in the present moment—there is no way of knowing that there ever was a past, or, even if there were, no way of knowing what sensations and ideas one might have had in that past.

As for the future, because it never exists in the present, there is no requirement to explain its existence in the present. As to where the notion of a future comes from, its only source is a projection from sensations and ideas in the present. From an imaginary past derived from memory-ideas that exist in present, one projects an imaginary

7

future consisting of sensations and ideas about a projected future, which sensations and ideas one is conscious of only in the present moment.

From one's sensations and ideas—all of which exist only in the present moment—the solipsist of the present moment can know only that he exists *only* as the consciousness of those sensations and ideas, only in the present moment. Precisely, the world of the solipsist of the present moment exists only for one moment, only for the present moment. There is no past and no future in the world of the solipsist of the present moment. The sense that there is a past and a future is an illusion derived from the sensations and ideas present to the solipsist's consciousness *at the present moment.*

Here is another way to consider this illusion of the passing of time. The notion of time passing derives from present consciousness of relations of succession among the sensations and ideas in the present set of one's sensations and ideas. Think of a length of movie film stretched out and observed all at once, with each successive frame sequentially providing the sense of having been perceived before the next frame. And yet—like the pictures in the movie film—all memories in any memory sequence exist only at the same time, the present moment, and thus provide no knowledge that any of them represent—and thus provide any knowledge of—any past consciousness. In other words, memories are deceptions. Only sensations and ideas experienced in the present moment can be known for certain to exist.

I am acutely aware that my attempt to explain how the solipsist's impression that there was a past—when only the present exists for the solipsist—may appear to be as inadequate, incoherent, and impermissible as I argue below in the chapter on Idealism that the Absolute or God of Idealists is inadequate, incoherent, and impermissible. My claim is that while the Idealists introduce magic with their notions of God and the Absolute, I am attempting to explain that something that actually does exist in empirical consciousness—the present memory ideas that apparently give reports of past experiences and events—do not refer to an actual past, but to an illusory past, because all that exists—the only thing for which there is empirical evidence that it exists—is the solipsist who is conscious in the present moment.

Where do the presently existing sensations, ideas, and pseudo-memories of the solipsist come from? They have no source of which the solipsist has any evidence. They just appear in the present moment. If this seems bothersome, it is only because one has accepted—without any grounds or proof—the notion that everything must have a cause. Both David Hume and Immanuel Kant also recognize that the notion that everything (or anything) has a cause cannot be proved. The notion of causation must be implicit in one's consciousness, or hypothesized.

Bertrand Russell offers as an objection to solipsism that he has knowledge of things he had to have gained from past experience. Russell is appealing to a common-sense view of the world, according to which memories provide reports of past experiences and events. But the solipsist has no evidence that a common-sense world exists, no knowledge that anything exists other than the ideas and sensations he is conscious of in the present moment.

Russell did take solipsism seriously as shown by his trying to refute it, but he never resolved his worries about it, and in *The Problems of Philosophy* (1912) he concludes as follows:

> In one sense it must be admitted that we [one] can never *prove* the existence of things other than ourselves [one's self] and our [one's] experiences. No logical absurdity results from the hypothesis that the world consists of myself and my thoughts and feelings and dreams and sensations, and that everything else is mere fancy. (p. 22)

Russell presumes—correctly—that he need say no more to lead most people to put solipsism aside. What Russell leaves unsaid is that in a lifetime of worrying about solipsism, and stating that it was not a threat, he also found no logical reason to suppose that it is false:

> There is no logical impossibility in the suggestion that the whole of life is a dream, in which we ourselves [I myself] create all the objects that come before us [me]. But although this is not logically impossible, there is no reason whatsoever to suppose that it is true; and it is, in fact, a less simple hypothesis, viewed as a means of accounting

9

for the facts of our [one's] own life, than the common-sense hypothesis that there really are objects independent of us [one], whose action on us [one] cause our [one's] sensations. (pp. 23–24)

Russell concludes by saying that:

All knowledge, we find [one finds], must be built up upon our [one's] instinctive beliefs, and if these are rejected, nothing is left. (p. 25)

Russell means that one's instinctive beliefs provide no reason in support of the existence of the common-sense world. He puts solipsism aside by stating that the common-sense view of the world is more simple than the solipsistic view, which, in fact, it is not. The world of common-sense is explained by science—physics, biology, etc.—but the world of the solipsist of the present moment neither has nor requires a cause nor an explanation. Momentary consciousness just is what it is.

Note well that this does not mean that solipsism of the present moment implies that one should or must give up the usefulness of operating as though a world of many conscious minds and of common-sense, material objects exists. As I discuss in a separate chapter below, the immaterialist George Berkeley proposed the utility for conscious minds of being able to maneuver in the fully immaterial world *as though* it consists of common-sense material bodies.

In the late eighteenth and early nineteenth centuries, Idealism (which I discuss in detail in a separate chapter below)—the general anti-materialist view that all that exists is mental and so we have direct knowledge or consciousness only of mental selves, ideas, and sensations—was held by many philosophers. For an Idealist, even if the material objects of common-sense realism should exist, one would have no direct access to them, and thus no direct knowledge of their characteristics or that they exist. And obviously with no direct way to verify the existence of the objects of common-sense realism, one can have no empirical proof that they do exist.

Most theories of Idealism derive to some important extent from Immanuel Kant's *Critique of Pure Reason* (first published in 1787)

(I also discuss Kant in a separate chapter below). Kant proposes that non-perceptible things in themselves are resolved in one's mind in spatio-temporal context according to categories of quantity, quality, modality, and relation, with the result being one's sensory perception and intellectual knowledge and experience of the world of common-sense. He stresses that there is no way of knowing if anything exists other than one's own private consciousness and understanding of this self-constructed world. This seems to be grounds for inference to solipsism, but perhaps because most Idealists are religious with faith in the Christian God, few of them ever considered the possibility of solipsism seriously. I examine the implications of Idealism for solipsism in a separate chapter below.

The realists Bertrand Russell and G. E. Moore did try to refute Idealism, but never succeeded, so finally they decided to ignore it, hoping it would go away. But (as I discuss in separate chapters below on Carnap and Goodman) with the rise of Logical Positivism in Anglo-American philosophy in the 1930s, solipsism did not go away. There is also a Wittgensteinian school of ordinary language philosophy according to which it is argued that ordinary common-sense language could never have developed if there were not a community of people speaking it in a common-sense world. But this reasoning from supposed implications of language to the actual existence of other minds and common-sense objects such as chairs (neither of which is directly perceptible) is to make an unjustified leap beyond one's sensory data to belief in other minds and common-sense objects. In some respects, this Wittgensteinian language-based argument against solipsism is a reverse image of the argument for solipsism of the present moment from the momentary awareness of sensations and ideas that I present above. The Wittgensteinians assume that there is a public, common-sense world of bodies and language speakers whose existence needs no proof. I argue that there is no proof that there exists anything other than one's conscious sensations and ideas in the present moment.

To complete this brief introduction to solipsism of the present moment, I note that virtually always when there is a reference to solipsism in the philosophical literature of the twentieth century, no serious effort is made either to explain the reasons for it, or to refute it. It is generally dismissed because it is not taken seriously.

When solipsism is seen to be a serious, but insoluble problem, it is often dismissed with a *non sequitur* joke, as Bertrand Russell does in his *An Outline of Philosophy* of 1927:

> I once received a letter from a philosopher who professed to be a solipsist, but was surprised that there were no others: Yet this philosopher was by way of believing that no one else existed. This shows that solipsism is not really believed even by those who think they are convinced of its truth. (p. 102)

It is not beyond the realms of possibility that Russell was being put on. This, in fact, is very likely, because the philosopher who wrote this letter to him was Christine Ladd-Franklin, who was known both for her logical acumen and for her wit and was not above tweaking Russell, who himself was known for taking himself very seriously. Russell's comment also illustrates the commonplace logical lapse exhibited in most proposed claims that solipsism must be false. The logical lapse is the assumption that other consciousnesses do exist—which is the point in contention—of which one has no proof.

A common such claim to refute solipsism is exemplified by Windleband in his famous *A History of Philosophy*, in which he states that "the solipsist refutes himself by beginning to prove his doctrine to others" (p. 472). But this claim is false. Even if the solipsist does propose to prove solipsism "to others," just because the solipsist might think that other conscious minds do, or might, exist, this does not mean that his belief and his attempt to argue with those fictitious others prove that any conscious being exists other than the solipsist himself. In fact, of course, if more than one solipsist did exist, each would be confined to his own manifold of self-consciousness, and could not communicate with any other, or have any way of knowing that any other exists. If there were more than one solipsist, each would be confined to his own private world of consciousness.

The champion defender of common-sense realism is the great common-sense philosopher, G. E. Moore. Moore came to the conclusion that solipsism, and in particular its denial of the existence of the common-sense material world, can not be refuted, but his reaction was not to propose an argument for the existence of the common-sense world, but to try to make solipsism look ridiculous. His most famous exercise in this line is his lecture "Proof of an External World," which features his holding up one hand and saying, "This is a hand," and then holding up the other and saying that it is a hand, too.

In the Fall of 1958, when I arrived as a graduate student at the University of Michigan, the great joke going around the philosophy department was that Moore had recently presented his "Proof of an External World" there. He held up a hand and said, "I'm as sure that this is a hand as I am that the sun is shining down through that sky-light," at which point he gestured to the large square of opaque glass in the center of the ceiling that illuminated the lecture room.

This lecture room is in a basement in a building several stories high.

So what? If anyone had been so impolite (or so daring) as to point this out to Moore, what would he have said? He would have smiled and very slightly shaken his head.

René Descartes (1596–1650)

René Descartes, the Father of Modern Philosophy, initiated the modern quest for certainty. But rather than making a list of what he knew for certain as other philosophers contemporary to him had done, Descartes instead asked himself what he could not doubt. He found that he could not doubt his own existence. His phrase, "*Cogito ergo sum*" translated as "I think, therefore I am" (*Discourse on the Method*, p. 127) (more literally translated as "I am thinking, therefore I am existing") is known to virtually everyone who has any knowledge of Western philosophy, and, in fact, it is known to vast numbers of people by familiarity with the hundreds of jokes exemplified by the cartoon of a dog saying, "I bark, therefore I am." If you know that you exist, then you are a self-conscious being who knows at least one item of certain knowledge: I am aware that I am thinking, therefore I exist.

Descartes is an ontological dualist who holds that only two kinds of substances exist: self-consciously thinking, un-extended, and self-activating minds on the one hand, and on the other, unconscious unthinking, extended, and inactive material bodies. This division between two substances—active mind and inactive body—gave rise to the classic mind-body problem: How can mental minds that are un-extended, active, conscious, have no solidity, and take up no space interact with material bodies that are extended, passive, non-conscious, solid, and take up space?

Despite the apparent impossibility of interaction between minds and bodies, they obviously do interact causally. One can mentally will to move one's material arm and it moves, and if one's material arm bumps the back of a chair, one has a mental sensation of pain.

How can two such oppositely different things—mind and body—interact?

On the traditional Cartesian definitions of mental mind and material body, there is no possible way mind and body can interact.

When Princess Elisabeth of Bohemia asked Descartes about this, Descartes said not to worry, God can make it happen. Nevertheless, because mind and body do interact, and because it is impossible without a miracle for a material thing (body) to causally interact with an immaterial thing (mind), virtually no philosopher today admits to being a Cartesian mind-body dualist.

Most non-philosophers—who do not think about it—are. Nevertheless, the mind-body problem—how to explain the interaction of a mind and a body—continues to worry philosophers and scientists in its traditional dualist form.

Also, the vast majority of people in the Western world are Cartesian dualists, if for no other reason because of Judaic, Christian, Moslem, and other religious beliefs about the survival of an immaterial human soul after the death and disintegration of the human body.

One attempt to solve this problem of the seeming impossibility of interaction between a material body and an immaterial soul is to deny the dualism of mind and matter, to assert either that only matter exists, so the mind is not mental but is material like the body, or to assert that only mind exists, so the body is not material but is mental like the mind. The one position is materialism. The other position is mentalism, of which the most well-developed form is Idealism. For an Idealist, all that exists is mental. Solipsism is a form of Idealism: For the solipsist, only his momentary self-conscious sensations and ideas exist. And as I argue above, these self-conscious sensations and ideas exist only in the present moment.

Most scientists today are materialists. They believe that everything in the universe is material in the current scientific meaning of that term, which goes far beyond Descartes's definition of material things simply as bodies that are extended in space. But it is in fact easier—because it raises fewer problems—to defend the view that everything in the universe is mental. This is because one has direct experience of mental things—ideas and sensations—whereas one does not have direct experience of material things, but can only postulate or infer that material things exist from the sensations and ideas that hypothetical bodies are assumed to cause.

Descartes was a mind-body dualist, as are most human beings. Most people believe that the world consists both of material bodies that are extended in space, and mental minds that are un-extended and do not exist in space. Thus the common-sense view of the world is dualist.

The dualist position that a human being consists of both a body and a mind, is essential for all religions in which it is believed that the soul—which is the conscious mind—is separated from the body at death and transported to heaven or survives the dissolution of the body in some other way. Because of this belief, people who believe in an after-life are not materialists. For this same reason, most materialist scientists are not religious. The materialist scientific viewpoint is that the mind (soul) is simply a manifestation of the material human body, and does not survive that body's death. Consequently, materialism is generally associated with atheism, whereas Idealism is generally associated with religious belief.

One accusation that might be made against a professed solipsist in the Cartesian tradition is that he is a megalomaniac who believes that he is God. If only the solipsist exists, then he is the only candidate for God. If there must be a cause of the solipsist's sensations and ideas—of his very existence—the only source for this cause is the solipsist himself. This surmise, however, that the solipsist is, or even thinks he is, God, is weakened by the fact that the solipsist does not have the super-natural powers traditionally attributed to God. Nothing indicates to the solipsist that he causes more than a very few of the sensations and ideas he has at the present moment. He can apparently cause a few of his sensations and ideas, but only a very few of those in the multitude of experiences that come to him without his being able either to cause them or guide them.

In fact, nothing indicates to the solipsist that the sensations and ideas he has even have a cause or must have a cause. All the solipsist knows, and all the solipsist has any evidence for, is that at the present moment he is conscious of an array of sensations and ideas.

Descartes never questioned the existence of either mental minds or material bodies. He was a good Catholic who believed that an immaterial, conscious (and thus mental) God created the world of material things. God also created each person's mind or immaterial soul. At this point, Descartes faced a problem. The essence of a human mind/soul is its thinking, its conscious continuous, active thinking, which he took to be an immaterial substance. Thus the existence of a human mind/soul depends on its continuously thinking. But one's experience is that there are many stretches of time during which one is not thinking—when one's mind is an inactive blank— particularly when one is in a deep sleep. In opposition to Descartes's theory of the existence of the human mind as a continuously conscious, thinking thing, it would thus seem that there are many periods of time during which one is not thinking, and so does not exist.

When I am thinking, I exist.

When I am not thinking, I do not exist.

According to Descartes, the solution to this problem is that often, particularly when one is asleep, one's conscious thoughts are so light and evanescent that they are diaphanous and fleeting. One forgets them the moment one has them. The result is that one has the false impression that there are stretches of time during which one has no thoughts at all. But according to Descartes, one is always thinking— to exist just is to be thinking—so when one has the impression that periods of time have gone by when one was not thinking, one was just having very light thoughts that one forgot as soon as one had them. This is how Descartes tries to preserve his ontological claim that the essence of mind is thinking, and thus that a mind must be conscious of its thinking all the time.

Of course one cannot test or verify this theory. If one does not remember being conscious all the time, there is no way to examine whether or not one actually is conscious all the time. But, on Descartes's theory, continual thinking is necessary for one's mind to exist at all: The mind must be consciously thinking all the time. So the appearance one has that one has not been thinking all the time *must* be the result of periods of sleep or unconsciousness during which one does not remember having thoughts one is really having— the result of serial, instantaneous forgetting. If one actually did not have conscious thoughts all the time, the conclusion would have to be that one does not exist all the time.

But so what? There is no reason why a solipsist must think—and thus exist—all the time. Gaps in the solipsist's consciousness, that is, in his existence, would not be noticed. In fact, however, given that the solipsist exists only in the present moment, he does not exist in time, and so there is no sense in which there could be gaps in his existence.

For a dualist who believes that the world consists of mental minds, substances that have ideas and sensations as properties, and of material bodies that have size, shape, and position as properties, what does the material world outside one's ideas and sensations consist of? The material world consists of bodies, of tables and chairs, trees, animals, rocks, earth, air, fire, water, and all the bodies one encounters in one's daily life. One also has explanations for why these bodies behave the way they do, for example, the law of falling bodies. This view of the material world is *naïve realism*. It is naïve because one takes it for granted and virtually never questions it. As for how bodies behave, this is knowledge those who practice the new science of physics (of which Descartes was a founder) investigate.

The new scientists contrast the ordinary bodies of naïve realism to those of *scientific realism*, the view that what really exists in the world are atoms, protons, neurons, sub-atomic particles, and so on—perhaps even strings and dark matter—entities that are material in the twenty-first-century sense. They are never known as extended bodies in direct perception as Descartes said they are; scientific objects are known only theoretically from what one infers from use of scientific instruments such as electron microscopes. Scientific objects are the entities referred to in scientific explanations. Their relations are explained by scientific laws, most of which are in the form of mathematical equations such as $e = mc^2$.

Advocates of naïve realism and of scientific realism use many arguments to defend the one against the other concerning what material objects "really" are. But there is no reason why they need conflict. Each serves its purpose in its place—naïve realism in ordinary life, scientific realism in scientific investigations. Both are based on empirical examinations of the world as human beings experience it. Nothing would change in the experience of human beings if it were really the case that the world of naïve realism were the real world, and the world of scientific realism just a mathematical construct. On the other hand, nothing would change in the experience of human beings if it were really the case that the world of scientific realism were the real world and the world of naïve realism just a crude construct derived from the interactions of the human body and brain with material things in the world.

As far as that goes, nothing would change in human experience if Idealism were true, and no material bodies existed. And—you saw it coming—the salient fact here, the point I am making, is that nothing would change in human experience if solipsism of the present moment is true.

This ultimate result has its origin in Western philosophy in the fact that nothing would change in human experience if Idealism—the ontological theory that everything in the world is mental, even bodies—were true. George Berkeley held the view that everything in the world is mental. And just as Descartes has been accused of being a solipsist because all he could apparently know for certain is "I think, therefore I am," Berkley was accused of being a solipsist because all he could know for certain is the existence of his own thoughts.

Before proceeding with George Berkeley, consider—that according both to naïve realism and to scientific realism—what a strange place the world is! So far as one knows from immediate experience, the world exists only in the present moment when one is perceiving it. That the world exists when it is not being perceived cannot be established with certainty. This bothered philosophers for so long that most Western philosophers today disdain the notion of, and the search for, absolute certainty, as though just because one cannot establish that the world exists when it is not being perceived, one is justified in dismissing the search for certainty entirely. But of course one does know something for certain, the sensations and ideas one has at the present moment.

One has absolute certainty—a lot of it—about one's own sensations and ideas at the present moment. It is true, however, that one does not know that one had any certainty in any past moment, nor even any certainty that there was a past moment. My foundational point here is that one certainly does not know if oneself existed in a past moment. But one does know that one exists—and the sensations and ideas one is conscious of—in the present moment.

My point here is that the very idea that bodies and minds persist or exist and pass through time is incomprehensible because the notion of time itself is incomprehensible.

It appears that bodies exist and pass through time. In fact, the notion that bodies change depends itself on the assumption that they pass through time. But time itself is an artifact hypothesized from the idea that bodies change. The perception of change is what supports the notion of passing time.

But—something Augustine worried about—*how* a body is present and passes through time—is not explained. In fact, the very notion that a body is an entity that travels through time is incomprehensible—as though time were eternally present like an ocean for bodies to swim through. But that makes time into something that remains the same through time while it also passes away moment by moment. This is a contradictory notion that makes no sense.

What a strange entity a body that persists through time is presumed to be, a thing that exists through time. Now it is, then it isn't, because the moment does not last—it has no temporal length. The body cannot be in the previous moment that no longer exists. Instead, it magically appears in the next moment, magically, but immediately that moment is gone and the body appears in the next moment, and so on. A body cannot persist through time, because there is no persisting time to pass through. A body apparently comes into, goes out of, and comes into existence, continuously, moment to moment.

Time is a very strange entity. So are bodies, for that matter—bodies that exist in one moment, vanish, and then exist in the next moment.

On the other hand, if bodies do not exist, and if all one perceives are momentary sensations and ideas, the enigma of how bodies persist through time is avoided. I go on now to George Berkeley who avoided the problems of mind-body dualism, of what matter could be, and of how bodies persist through time, by denying that bodies exist at all.

The unsurprising result of this trajectory down the memory lane of Modern philosophy is reduction to the solipsism of the present moment.

George Berkeley (1685–1753)

In the "Introduction" to her collection of writings by George Berkeley (1929), Mary Whiton Calkins mentions in passing Berkeley's "unwitting solipsism" (Calkins, p. li). This comment, which she obviously believes needs no support or explication, derives from Berkeley's Idealism. As opposed to Descartes's dualism of two substances, mental and material, Berkeley argues that only one kind of substance exists: All that exists is mental, consisting of minds and the mental sensations and ideas of which these minds are conscious. An infinitely powerful God creates and sustains the finite minds of individual human beings. God also maintains a universe of sensations and ideas that human minds perceive. Perceptually, nothing in this mental world appears any different from the way it would appear if the world consisted of Descartes's dualistic world of material bodies and mental minds interacting with one another, because Descartes cannot perceive material bodies. Descartes can perceive only mental sensations and ideas, just like Berkeley.

Structurally, Berkeley's monism represents a way of eliminating the problems of Descartes's dualism. Interactions between mind and matter do not pose a problem when matter is eliminated and both minds and bodies are mental. God, being Himself a mental substance, and all-powerful, can easily cause human minds to have sensations and ideas that appear to derive from and represent a world of material bodies. According to Berkeley, this appearance that sensations and ideas are caused by material bodies is only an illusion. Why God chooses to perpetuate this illusion is not explained.

Berkeley begins *A Treatise Concerning The Principles of Human Knowledge* as follows:

> It is evident to any one who takes a survey of the *objects of human knowledge*, that they are either *ideas* actually imprinted on the senses; or else such as are perceived by

21

attending to the passions and operations of the mind; or lastly, *ideas* formed by the help of memory and imagination—either compounding, dividing, or barely representing those originally perceived in the aforesaid ways. (p. 124)

He continues that

collections of ideas constitute a stone, a tree, a book, and the like sensible things [and there is] something which knows or perceives them; and exercises divers operations, as willing, imagining, remembering about them. This perceiving, active being is what I call *mind, spirit, soul*, or myself. By which words I do not denote any one of my ideas, but a thing entirely distinct from them, wherein they exist, or which is the same thing, whereby they are perceived; for the existence of an idea constitutes in being perceived. (pp. 124–25)

Thus the phrase of Berkeley: *To be, is to be perceived*, which is almost as well-known as Descartes's: *I think, therefore I am.*

One cannot proceed here without mentioning the "refutation" of Berkeley by the famous Dr. Johnson. The story goes that Dr. Johnson kicked a stone, and said, "Thus I refute Berkeley." What he actually did, of course, was demonstrate his own pig-headed stupidity concerning Berkeley's philosophy. According to Berkeley, just as God provided visual images of the stone, God also provided Dr. Johnson the feeling of solidity when Dr. Johnson caused himself to have the ideas of kicking the stone. I include this story for more than amusement. Every rejection of solipsism I know of exhibits this kind of know-nothing determination to understand neither the position of, nor the arguments for, solipsism. Or, as the Logical Positivist Gustav Bergmann does, solipsism is just fobbed off:

I happen to believe that there are, in some sense, mental states numerically different from my own, yet it is not necessary to complicate the present discussion by introducing into it the puzzles connected with the belief in the existence of other minds. Whatever the solution of those puzzles is,

22

> I do know at least that *I* do have mental states and that my "having" them is a fact different from—though, of course, not causally unrelated to—the facts mentioned in a behavioristic analysis of my having them. (*The Metaphysics of Logical Positivism*, pp. 218–19)

Bergmann's retreat from and dismissal of what he would have referred to as the "slippery slope" to solipsism from any discussion of mental states is typical of sense-datum philosophers. But if they begin with private sense-data, as Bergmann does, they cannot avoid the slippery slope to solipsism. So they just dismiss or ignore it. I discuss this in the chapters on Rudolf Carnap and Nelson Goodman below.

What Calkins means by Berkeley's "unwitting solipsism" is that if one subtracts God from his metaphysical system—and of course there is no evidence in sensory experience for the existence of God—one has direct evidence only for existence of one's own sensations and ideas. Atheist philosophers just dispense with God. For example, David Hume, whose solipsism derives from Berkeley's immaterialism, makes fun of the notion of an all-powerful God in his *Dialogues Concerning Natural Religion* by suggesting that the world is in such a mess that God may have created it when he was an infant, or when he was senile, or—horror of horrors—maybe God is a committee (pp. 36–38).

In his *Principles of Human Knowledge* of 1710, Berkeley eliminates the possibility that there are material things that exist unperceived by saying that when you

> imagine trees, for instance, in a park, or books existing in a closet, and nobody by to perceive them . . . do not you yourself perceive or think of them all the while? . . . To make out this, it is necessary that you conceive them existing unconceived or unthought of; which is a manifest repugnancy. (p. 136)

To the objection that this means that ideas, and thus the entire universe, have existence only when being perceived by someone, Berkeley responds that the entire world of sensations is perceived by God, "that Active Principle and wise Spirit 'in whom we live, move, and have our being'" (p. 161). God is the supreme spirit who is all-powerfully active, but each of us, each mind, also is (finitely) active:

> All the unthinking objects [sensations and ideas] of the mind agree in that they are entirely passive, and their existence consists only in being perceived: whereas a *soul* or *spirit* is an active being, whose existence consists, not in being perceived, but in perceiving ideas and thinking. (p. 205)

One knows of the existence of other souls and spirits including God only by inference from one's "direct and immediate view" of one's own mind:

> As we conceive the ideas that are in the minds of other spirits by means of our own, which we suppose to be resemblances of them, so we know other spirits [including God] by means of our own soul; which in that sense is the image or idea of them. (p. 206)

It is easy to see what havoc a skeptic like Hume can make of Berkeley's brilliant, but naïve, exposition of one's immediate consciousness of sensations and ideas. For Berkeley, as for Hume, one has immediate knowledge only of sensations and ideas in the present moment. And all that one can claim to know for certain is what one experiences in the present moment. So Berkeley's Idealism (like the British Idealisms of the nineteenth century) is set up for stripping down, as Hume does, to the momentary-subject solipsism of the present moment.

Most damaging to Berkeley's position is that there is no need to postulate any cause for sensations and ideas. They simply appear in one's consciousness. One does not perceive any cause—such as God—of them. So there is neither any evidence for, nor any need for God in Berkeley's system. God can be eliminated from Berkeley's system (as David Hume does from his) the same way Berkeley himself eliminated material bodies from his system: there is no evidence for their existence in conscious experience. That is, one never perceives either bodies or God.

With no proof of God's existence, one's perceptions and ideas have—and need—no cause. They are just there. Thus our sensations and ideas do not need a mind to support them. One's own mind is nothing more than a collection of immediately conscious sensations and ideas. A mind that persists through time thus is just like one's body, a hypothetical entity constructed from one's sensations and ideas. Neither God, minds, nor bodies actually exist. All that exists are sensations and ideas.

Finally, there is no evidence that any other minds or consciousnesses exist other than one's own. This consciousness exists only in the present moment, so Berkeley's position quickly reduces to solipsism of the present moment.

David Hume makes this explicit.

David Hume (1711–1776)

David Hume agrees with Descartes that one's existence depends on one's being conscious of one's perceptions, which he calls impressions and ideas, and which he distinguishes in his *Treatise of Human Nature* of 1739 as follows:

> All the perceptions of the human mind resolve themselves into two distinct kinds, which I shall call IMPRESSIONS and IDEAS. The difference betwixt these consists in the degrees of force and liveliness with which they strike upon the mind. Those perceptions, which enter with most force and violence, we may name *impressions*; and under this name I comprehend all our sensations, passions, and emotions, as they make their first appearance in the soul. By *ideas* I mean the faint images of these in thinking and reasoning. (p. 1)

These impressions and ideas include everything that, and only what, one can have in consciousness, from sensations and passions to concepts and images—everything one can experience, imagine, and think about.

Descartes assumes without criticism that one's mind (and thus consciousness) and body (and all other material things) are substances that persist through time. Hume points out that in fact there is no evidence that such things as minds and bodies exist, and plenty of evidence that even if they do exist, they do not persist through time. Thus Hume attacks Descartes's uncritical acceptance of the view that the world consists of two substances and their properties. For Descartes, material bodies have size, shape, and position; mental minds have sensations and ideas. But, Hume points out, one never has direct perception either of bodies or of minds. Nor is one conscious of the properties of bodies, such as their size and shape. One is conscious only of such properties as feelings of hardness and expanses of color. Also, one is never conscious of minds, but only of sensations and ideas. One never encounters minds or bodies directly. One simply infers that minds and bodies exist on the basis of experiencing sensations and ideas. But without direct contact either with bodies or with a mind, but rather only with sensations and ideas, one cannot know for certain that bodies exist or even that one's mind exists as an independent substance that has the sensations and ideas one experiences. All that one knows immediately and thus certainly to exist are the sensations and ideas of which one has direct consciousness in the present moment. Thus one has no certain knowledge that one's being—as consciously experienced—exists at any time other than in the present moment that one senses one's sensations and one understands one's ideas.

Thus, Hume denies Descartes's claim that one's sensations and ideas belong to a mind. For Hume, a mind is not a substance that endures through time, but rather a mind consists simply of a collection of conscious sensations and ideas that exist at the present moment. Obviously, this mind—a collection of conscious sensations and ideas that exist in the present moment—is solipsistic.

> What we call a *mind*, is nothing but a heap or collection of different perceptions, united together by certain relations, and supos'd, tho' falsely, to be endow'd as separately existent. (p. 207)

To separate his philosophic speculations from his ordinary life of playing whist with his men friends and cavorting with his lady friends—he was a plump jolly man and very popular—Hume once said that he did philosophy in the closet. (Hume had a coarse enough sense of humor to make one wonder which closet he had in mind.) Hume never said he was a solipsist, although his entire metaphysical position is solipsistic. My thesis is that Hume was a closet solipsist.

Descartes believes that in one's mind, one has records in the form of memories of experiences of sensations and ideas one had in the past. But for Hume, these memories are illusory. Hume points out that all these memories are in fact sensations experienced and ideas understood in the present moment, all of which have about them a felt aura of pastness. The content of these memories also have an aura of being in a sequential temporal order of past occurrence.

27

This felt aura of sequential pastness makes a press of memory sensations and ideas that exist in the present moment of consciousness appear to refer sequentially to a receding sequence of past experiences of sensations and ideas. Each memory sensation or idea in the sequence is of events that seemingly happened farther and farther back in the past. But in fact, all these memories are being experienced now, at the present moment, and the sense they give of reporting experiences one had in the past is an illusion. The sense of passing time is an illusion, not in how it appears, but in what one takes it to be an appearance of, that is, of real passing time. But one's perceptions are always present perceptions of present sensations and ideas.

Thus this aura of pastness does not confirm that memories actually do record a temporal sequence of past experiences. No matter how intense one's sense is that these memories are records of temporal sequences of past experiences, all memories exist in one's present consciousness. Just because they seem to be records of past experiences, they do not themselves exist in the past. Nor is there any way to confirm (or disconfirm) that there ever was a past sequence of experiences or events such as those the present memories seem to record. One cannot go back to past time to test or to confirm the claim that any events at all actually occurred in the past.

> When we search for the characteristic, which distinguishes the *memory* from the imagination, we must immediately perceive, that it cannot lie in the simple ideas it presents to us; since both these facilities borrow their simple ideas from the impressions, and can never go beyond these original perceptions. These faculties are as little distinguish'd from each other by the arrangement of their complex ideas. For tho' it be a peculiar property of the memory to preserve the original order and position of its ideas, while the imagination transposes and changes them, as it pleases; yet this difference is not sufficient to distinguish them in their operation, or to recal the past impressions, in order to compare them with our present ideas, and see whether their arrangement be exactly similar. (p. 85)

So could one have come into existence now at the present

moment, with all one's memories in place, although one had no past experiences at all? Yes. Could it even be the case that nothing at all was in existence before this moment? Yes. And could it be that the only existence there is, was, and ever will be is one's conscious experience of it at this moment? Yes.

For Hume, the sense of existing through time can only be an illusion. His views exactly support the solipsism of the present moment implication that all that exists, and all that has existed or ever will exist, is the conscious bundle of sensations and ideas existing at the present moment. And for Hume, in that present moment one is conscious of some sensations and ideas that have a false, misleading aura of being memories of actual past events. All the contents of memories exist only in the present and have no external referents.

Similarly, Hume points out that one recognizes that the imagined sensations and ideas that one anticipates having in the future are imagined only in the present and do not refer to any actual sensations and ideas that will exist in the future. Just as the past never existed, the future does not exist, and never will. No matter how future-oriented imagined sensations and ideas are or appear to be, these imagined sensations and ideas concerning the future exist—like imagined past sensations and ideas—only in one's present consciousness. All that one knows for certain to exist are the sensations and ideas one perceives in the present moment.

All one's experience leads to the conclusion that Hume is right. One generally thinks of oneself as a material body that is conscious some of the time. One is not ordinarily conscious when one is asleep, and sometimes one is not conscious when one is awake. But one believes that one's body persists through passing time, whether or not one's mind is conscious. At some point after one is born, memories of one's conscious thoughts and bodily behavior begin to accumulate, and from then on one thinks of oneself as a coherent, persisting entity—a conscious human being with a persisting mind and a persisting body.

One ordinarily presumes that one's mind and body persist even though both one's body and mind change over the years. As for the human body, its material constituents are (so it is generally said) completely replaced in a period of seven years. Does one's basic mind pattern similarly persist? Maybe not. If the identity of a mind depends on its continuity of memories (as one's body depends on a continuity of form) then a mind can be eliminated by being completely emptied of memories by Alzheimer's disease—while the body remains.

But for Hume the notion that one has a body is an illusion:

> Nothing is ever really present with the mind but its percep-
> tions or impressions and ideas . . . 'tis impossible for us
> so much as to conceive or form an idea of anything specif-
> ically different from ideas and impressions. Let us fix our
> attention out of ourselves as much as possible: Let us chace
> our imagination to the heavens, or to the utmost limits of
> the universe; we never really advance a step beyond our-
> selves, nor can conceive any kind of existence, but those
> perceptions which have appear'd in that narrow compass.
> This is the universe of the imagination, nor have we any
> idea but what is there produc'd. (pp. 67–68)

> As to the notion of external existence [of bodies], when
> taken for something specifically different from our percep-
> tions, we have already shewn its absurdity. (p. 188)

All that exists for Hume are conscious sensations and ideas in the present moment. And this present moment could be the only moment that ever exists. That is, one can never confirm that one existed in the past because one's memories can never be checked. Of course one has the sense that time is passing. But one is conscious of one's sense of existing only in the present moment, and the present moment could be the only moment that one is ever conscious. If existence depends on consciousness, as Hume believes, then all that exists are the impressions and ideas one is experiencing in the present moment.

Hume, then, solipsistically challenges the view that a human being consists of a temporally enduring mind-body dualism of sub-stances. A conscious human being consists, Hume says, only of the bundle of sensory impressions and intelligible ideas of which one is conscious in the present moment.

There are all sorts of apparent records of one's past thoughts and bodily behavior—diaries, notes, films—that one can consult to check one's memories—but all of these records exist in the present. Even if they do report events that happened in the past, the reports them-selves are second-hand, divorced from the actual thoughts and expe-riences one had when one was conscious of having them. They are purported records that can never be confirmed by examining the past occurrences they purportedly record.

Nevertheless, it is of course important to try to find out whether or not one's memories of the past are, or can be, verified.

Consider standard scientific experimental practice. One hypothe-sizes that water will put out fire. To test this, one pours a glass of water onto a lighted candle. Not many tests are required for one to conclude that water will put out fire. Of course from scientific exper-iments, one can never conclude anything with absolute certainty—there is always uncertainty about the veracity of the reports and about what might happen next time—but science progresses by accepting provisional conclusions. A scientist builds theories on the basis of such provisional conclusions, of which the body of scientific theory is constructed, which conclusions are generally challenged only in exceptional circumstances.

Similarly, one's belief about one's conscious experiences in the past is tested by hypothesizing what one would be experiencing in the present moment if what one's memories of conscious experiences in the past are true of what actually did happen in the past. One builds up a belief in a body of consistent past experiences. But consistency itself is far from being an adequate criterion of veracity. It can be pro-posed as necessary, but the provision that consistency is necessary for bodies of experiences is itself a feature that cannot be checked. One simply cannot go back to examine conscious experiences again. There is no way to check whether or not one's present conscious memories of past experiences are true to those past experiences.

This fact about human experience is commonplace. For example, an enormous amount of litigation is based on just this point, on determining what actually did happen in the past. In a court of law, everyone agrees that any claim about what happened in the past can always be challenged. Nothing concerning what happened in the past can be established with absolute certainty. Memories of the past by litigants are especially vulnerable to inaccuracy. It is commonplace that memories of childhood, or even of what one had for breakfast, are susceptible not just to memory lapses or unconscious elaboration, but also to exaggeration, deletion, or fabrication.

This uncertainty about memories is so well-known that one just factors it (often automatically) into one's present beliefs about one's own past and one's evaluation of what others tell one about their own past experiences. Or, not always. Some people believe that their memories are infallible, sometimes even in the face of obvious contradictions. But memoirs and autobiographies are notoriously full of inaccuracies that stem sometimes from conscious dissimulations but just as often, or even more often, from faulty memories, or just from filling in the gaps with plausible fabrications. In fact, as a general rule, one's memory is always faulty. One simply cannot take everything in, so one cuts and fills to make one's experiences coherent.

Cutting and filling is demonstrated in law school classes with the favorite trick of having two men burst into classroom, one with a knife. They tussle, wrestle, and fall out the door that closes behind them. Then thirty students are asked to write down what they saw. You know the result—thirty different stories. Some will swear that they saw—and now remember—that the black man had the knife. Others that the white man had the knife. But it was not even a knife, it was a twelve-inch ruler. The two men were both black, or both white. And so on.

I make so much of this because even though one knows perfectly well about the uncertainty of memories, one so often ignores or forgets how uncertain they are—because one's mind is shot through with faulty memories. One lives in a world where many false memories are accepted as true. This means that one is totally accustomed to accepting memories as true that are always false to some extent and sometimes greatly different from what actually happened.

All this leads to the question: What makes you think that anything at all happened to you in the past? What evidence do you have that you did not come into being just at this moment, with all your memories?

Because you would be crazy if you thought that?

No. This is a serious philosophical investigation. The question of the nature of human existence, of what it is to be a conscious human being, is important. The idea that one exists only in the present moment is not crazy if it makes sense as a possibility. And it does. There is no way for certain to establish that one, with all one's memories, did not come into existence at just this moment, with a purported memory of previous moments. One exists always in the present. Solipsism is the view that one exists only in the present moment.

For Hume, the notion that one has a body and a mind is an illusion. All that exists for Hume are conscious sensations and ideas in the present moment. And this present moment could be the only moment—and you the only consciousness—that ever exists.

Hume's analysis of one's consciousness and its contents as existing in the present moment is the best that has ever been given. No, he does not lay it out as precisely as I do above. But it is there in his *Treatise*: The self is nothing but a bundle of perceptions and ideas existing in the present moment. In one of his most famous passages, Hume says:

> For my part, when I enter most intimately into what I call *myself*, I always stumble on some particular perception or other, of heat or cold, light or shade, love or hatred, pain or pleasure. I never can catch *myself* at any time without a perception, and never can observe any thing but the perception. When my perceptions are remov'd for any time, as by sound sleep; so long am I insensible of *myself*, and may truly be said not to exist. And were all my perceptions remov'd by death, and cou'd I neither think, nor feel, nor see, nor love, nor hate after the dissolution of my body, I shou'd be entirely annihilated, nor do I conceive what is farther requisite to make me a perfect non-entity. (p. 252)

The thesis of which I give an exposition above is presented this way:

> The mind is a kind of theatre, where several perceptions successively make their appearance; pass, re-pass, glide away, and mingle in an infinite variety of postures and situations. There is properly no *simplicity* in it at one time, nor *identity* in different: whatever natural propensity we

may have to imagine that simplicity and identity. The comparison of the theatre must not mislead us. They are the successive perceptions only, that constitute the mind; nor have we the most distant notion of the place, where these scenes are represented, or of the materials, of which it is compos'd. (p. 253)

This is followed by a profession of solipsism of the present moment:

Experience is a principle, which instructs me in the several conjunctions of objects for the past. Habit is another principle, which determines me to expect the same for the future; and both of them conspiring to operate upon the imagination, make me form certain ideas in a more intense and lively manner, than others, which are not attended with the same advantages. Without this quality, by which the mind enlivens some ideas beyond others (which seemingly is so trivial, and so little founded on reason) we cou'd never assent to any argument, nor carry our view beyond those few objects, which are present to our senses. Nay, even to these objects we cou'd never attribute any existence, but what was dependent on the senses; and must comprehend them entirely in that success of perceptions, which constitutes our self or person. Nay farther, even with relation to that succession, we cou'd only admit of those perceptions, which are immediately present to our consciousness, nor cou'd those lively images, with which the memory presents us, be ever receiv'd as true pictures of past perceptions. The memory, senses, and understanding are, therefore, all of them founded on the imagination, or the vivacity of our ideas. (p. 265)

Is *self* the same with *substance*? If it be, how can that question have place, concerning the substance of self, under a change of substance? If they be distinct, what is the difference betwixt them? For my part, I have a notion of neither, when conceiv'd distinct from particular perceptions.

Philosophers begin to be reconcil'd to the principle, *that we have no idea of external substance, distinct from the ideas of particular qualities.* This must pave the way for a like principle with regard to the mind, *that we have no notion of it, distinct from the particular perceptions.* (p. 635, Hume's italics)

Some readers will be impatiently objecting that Hume does not come right out and say that he is a solipsist. So what? What I demonstrate here is that Hume's skepticism leads to and supports solipsism, the solipsistic view that nothing exists, neither mind nor body, except particular perceptions—sensations and ideas—perceived in the present moment.

But was Hume really a solipsist? He certainly knew the thesis of solipsism. As I demonstrate—and there are many more passages in the *Treatise* I could quote to this end—a great many of Hume's theses support solipsism. But Hume was nothing if not devious. Above all, Hume was a humorist. He jokes throughout the *Treatise*. It is inconceivable that he did not purposely walk the tight wire above the abyss of solipsism.

Solipsism is not a crazy theory. The solipsistic stance is a realistic description of human existence. One is conscious, and thus one can be certain that one exists, only in the present moment.

Think about it this way. Just thinking about it in ordinary commonsense language, there will come for you a conscious moment that is exactly like the conscious moment you are having at the present time. It will be your last conscious moment. It will be the last moment you will be conscious before you die, before you go out of existence. It will be a conscious moment (like the present one) into which all you are, all your conscious being, is compressed. It will be what you are. Life will last an instant, and then be gone.

Immanuel Kant (1724–1804)

The foundational quest of Modern Philosophy is the search for certainty. The major results derive primarily from the metaphysical positions of René Descartes, George Berkeley, and David Hume. Each of these philosophers bases his philosophy on what he believes is certain knowledge, and in each case this is derived from immediate conscious experience.

As Descartes pursues this quest, he bases his attainment of certain knowledge on the epistemological principle or claim that only when one is consciously thinking does one know for certain that one exists—as a thinking thing: *cogito ergo sum*. Descartes is quite explicit about the content and temporal extent of this certain knowledge. He says that he is certain that he exists as a thinking thing only when—during the time that—he is conscious that he is thinking. This certainty pertains, then, only in that moment of self-consciousness, and during that moment, all Descartes knows for certain is that he exists as a thinking thing at that moment.

Thus, Descartes's *cogito ergo sum* is the foundation in Modern Philosophy of solipsism of the present moment. Strictly speaking, Saint Augustine had earlier come to the same conclusion about the certainty of one's being in the present moment of consciousness. Descartes read Augustine, but it is unknown whether or not Descartes took his *cogito ergo sum* from Augustine.

What, ontologically, does this momentary consciousness amount to? For Descartes, it is simply thought or thinking, an unextended substance that, along with the extended substance, matter, constitutes Descartes's ontological dualism, which dualism leads to the metaphysical problem of how unextended minds could possibly interact with extended bodies, a problem that continues to bother philosophers to the present day.

One solution to the mind-body problem was proposed by George Berkeley, who denies the existence of material things on the grounds that one has direct, certain knowledge only of one's own immediate experience of mental sensations and ideas. That is, a mental self knows only itself and its mental sensations and ideas. In fact, Berkeley claimed, one can make no sense of the notion that matter—of which no one is or can be conscious—exists. All one knows for certain to exist are mental sensations and ideas in one's own mind. The world of sensations and ideas that one inhabits is provided, according to Berkeley, by God.

David Hume drives this mentalism or idealism to its ultimate limit by stressing that one can have certainty only of the existence of one's own conscious thoughts—sensations and ideas—and of them only in one's own immediate consciousness, that is, as immediately conscious. But these immediately conscious thoughts are not, as they are for Descartes and Berkeley, immediately conscious to oneself as properties or qualifications of one's mind, for these conscious thoughts do not exist as properties or qualifications of anything—they exist only in themselves. They are not immediately conscious to, or as aspects of, a thinking thing or a conscious mind, but are simply conscious in themselves. Consciousness is their mode of being—just as for Descartes, extension is the mode of being of material bodies. In fact, for Hume the only things that exist are conscious sensations and ideas. This needs to be stressed, because some people argue that there cannot be a conscious sensation or idea unless there is a conscious mind to have them. Hume recognizes the reasoning behind this contention, but simply points out that he is restricting his acceptance of what he knows for certain only to what he is or can be conscious of—and he is conscious only in the present moment. And he has never been conscious of a mind that is purportedly conscious of sensations and ideas. Sensations and ideas apparently exist in themselves.

The result of this extreme search for certainty in Modern Philosophy, then, is that according to Descartes, Berkeley, and Hume, all that can be known for certain is what one is immediately conscious of in the present moment. Descartes and Berkeley claim that what one is immediately conscious of (and thus certainly exists) is a thinking or conscious thing—one's own mind or self—and the immediate sensations and ideas that are the contents of that thinking or conscious thing in the present moment. For Hume, immediately conscious sensations and ideas are the only things that exist. These conscious sensations and ideas do not belong to or exist in or qualify a consciousness, conscious substance, or a mind, as they do for Descartes and Berkeley. Hume's ontology contains no substances. Hume's sensations and ideas are simply conscious in themselves; for Hume, there are no minds that are conscious of sensations and ideas. There are only conscious sensations and ideas.

And these conscious sensations and ideas exist in, are known by experience to exist in, and only in, the present moment.

In sum, the reasoning that leads from the Cartesian stress in Modern philosophy on the private, immediately certain knowledge that one exists—and the result of focusing on the fact that one has this certain knowledge only of the sensations and ideas one is conscious of in the present moment—leads to solipsism of the present moment.

The major and most thoroughgoing attempt to avoid the solipsistic implications of Descartes's *cogito ergo sum* is that of Immanuel Kant in his *Critique of Pure Reason* (1781, 2nd ed. 1787) and *Prolegomena to Any Future Metaphysics That Will be Able to Come Forward as Science* (1783). In the *Critique*, Kant states his goal as that of determining "what and how much can the understanding know apart from all experience?" (*Critique* 12) He continues that

> we have no concepts of understanding, and consequently no elements for the knowledge of things . . . no knowledge of any object as thing in itself, but only in so far as it is an object of sensible intuition . . . an appearance. . . . [A]ll possible speculative knowledge of reason is limited to mere objects of *experience*. (*Critique* 27)

Despite this being the case, Kant boldly announces that

> I am just as certainly conscious that there are things outside me, which are in relation to my sense, as I am conscious that I myself exist as determined in time. . . . (*Critique* 36)

Kant's claims to have certain consciousness knowledge that there are things outside him, i.e., outside his sensations, and that his sensory experience is related to external things, and that he himself exists determined in time—are totally unsupported, and as brilliant and useful as his *Critique* is, he has no grounds for claiming that it is true of the—or of an—existing world independent of one's present consciousness.

I am not, by the way, making the ridiculous claim that Kant is not aware of these restrictions on his project, and of their solipsistic implications, or that he is trying to conceal them. As for solipsism, he says outright:

> We cannot judge in regard to the intuitions of other thinking beings [if there are other thinking beings], whether they are bound by the same conditions as those which limit our intuitions and which for us are universally valid. (*Critique* 72)

This point—that Kant makes clear that he knows perfectly well that he has no knowledge, let alone proof, that his analyses apply to a public world of other minds external to his private consciousness—is so important because Kant's *Critique* is a most influential analytic examination of human reason in the philosophical literature. And his candor is striking as he says early in his exposition:

> objects in themselves are quite unknown to us . . . what we call outer objects are nothing but mere representations of our sensibility, the form of which is space. The true correlate of sensibility, the thing in itself, is not known, and cannot be known, through these representations. . . . [As for time,] Time is not an empirical concept that has been derived from all intuitions . . . [it is] given *a priori*. . . . (*Critique* 74–75)

Thus Kant's procedure in meeting the threat of being confined only to his own perceptions and ideas is to admit it, and to proceed boldly and outright as though it makes no difference.

> To avoid all misapprehension, it is necessary to explain, as clearly as possible, what our view is regarding the fundamental constitution of sensible knowledge in general.

What we have meant to say is that all our intuition is nothing but the representation of appearance; that the things which we intuit are not in themselves what we intuit them as being, nor their relations so constituted in themselves as they appear to us, and that if the subject, or even only the subjective constitution of the senses in general, be removed, the whole constitution and all the relations of objects in space and time, nay space and time themselves, would vanish. As appearances, they cannot exist in themselves, but only in us. *What objects may be in themselves, and apart from all this receptivity of our sensibility, remains completely unknown to us. We know nothing but our mode of perceiving them.* (*Critique* 82, italics added)

In this context, most striking is Kant's discussion of the Cartesian *cogito ergo sum*, which supports the argument that the *cogito* leads to the solipsism of the present moment.

Certainly, the representation "I am", which expresses the consciousness that can accompany all thought, immediately includes in itself the existence of a subject. . . . (*Critique* 246)

More precisely,

Descartes was justified in limiting all perception, in the narrowest sense of that term, to the proposition, 'I, as a thinking thing, exist.' Obviously, since what is without is not me, I cannot encounter it in my apperception, nor therefore in any perception. . . . I am not, therefore, in a position to *perceive* external things, but can only infer their existence from my inner perception, taking the inner perception as the effect of which something external is the proximate cause. (*Critique* 345)

Kant supports Descartes in Descartes's inference to the existence of things external as the cause of inner perception, which is the position Kant himself holds. Finally, again, I point out that Kant does this on the basis of no concrete justification at all. That is, Kant's entire claim for the reality of his system of categories and interrelations is its applicability and completeness as an outline of human knowledge. There is no denying its brilliance and apparent completeness. There is, however, other than its structural perfection, no justification whatsoever for claiming—as Kant is careful not to do—that there is any proof—other than its applicability to appearances—that his categorical system describes the, or an, actual, existing world.

Does this really matter? I don't know.

What I am stressing is that the basic principle of the solipsism of the present moment is that the solipsist cannot accept the view that anything (particularly, himself, his own self-conscious being) exists other than what he is conscious of in the present moment—that is, his conscious sensations and ideas at that moment. The existence of anything else, including his own existence at an other time than the present moment is hypothetical only.

Kant recognizes the awkwardness of referring to oneself in any other way than as a conscious being or a consciousness. He speaks of

> the simple, and in itself completely empty representation 'I'; and we cannot even say that this is a concept, but only that it is a bare consciousness which accompanies all concepts. Through this I or he or it (the thing) which thinks, nothing further is represented than a transcendental subject of the thoughts = X. It is known only through the thoughts that are its predicates, and of it, apart from them, we cannot have any concept whatsoever. . . . [C]onsciousness in itself is not a representation distinguishing a particular object, but a form of representation in general, that is, of representation in so far as it is to be entitled knowledge; for it is only of knowledge that I can say that I am thereby thinking something. (*Critique* 331–32)

I present this passage at length to support my contention that in his exposition of the "transcendental subject of the thoughts = *I*," Kant makes patently clear that he does not know what he is talking about—he is saying that he does *not* know *what*, what entities or existents, he is talking about. His claim throughout the *Critique* to be giving an objective analysis of logical structure and content of human thought in general is unsupported. Granted that his critique of pure reason has application to the concepts and logical structure of human thought. What it does not do is expose a framework and content that can be proved to be—and often cannot be made intelligible as—the existing content of human thought and knowledge.

I am perfectly aware that in his torturous way, Kant is saying exactly this himself. What he does not admit outright is that he does not, and cannot, prove that there exists a world of objects outside his own present consciousness, a world structured as he describes it in his *Critique*.

I revert again to the ground of solipsism that stems from Descartes's quest in his *Meditations*, the search for certain knowledge. And I argue that in all of Kant's brilliant—and pertinent—analyses and expositions of the structure of human thought, he presents nothing that establishes the existence of anything but the consciousness of a set, *the* conscious set of the ideas and sensations possessed by the solipsist at the present moment.

Kant provides the foundation for solipsism of the present moment by such comments as

> The objects of experience . . . are *never* given *in themselves*, and have no existence outside it [i.e., outside one's own private, immediate experience]. (*Critique* 440)

Kant never claims that his categories apply to the world as it really is. He does not even claim that he knows for certain that there are minds other than his own. He simply provides a categorical analysis of the world as he experiences it.

Unfortunately, however, Kant's caveats were ignored and his *Critique* became the source of a metaphysical school of dogmatic religious idealism.

Idealism

Idealism in Western philosophy was developed in the eighteenth and nineteenth centuries on the ontological foundations of the monistic mentalism of George Berkeley in the course of the quest for certainty initiated by René Descartes. I show above how in that quest solipsism of the present moment derived from Descartes's *cogito ergo sum*, the full implication of which is: "I exist only when I am consciously thinking, and I am conscious that I am thinking only in the present moment." Descartes does not follow out the solipsistic implications of his *cogito*, but proposes instead a dualistic ontology consisting of mental minds and material bodies. This ontological dualism leads to the problem that plagues philosophers (and now neuroscientists) to the present day, of how immaterial minds and material bodies can possibly interact.

Berkeley bypasses this mind-body problem by arguing that one can know for certain that something exists only by having conscious awareness of it. One has conscious awareness only of mental things: minds, sensations, and ideas. One does not have conscious awareness of bodies, but dualists infer their existence as the cause of our sensations and ideas. Berkeley, however, concludes that because there is no direct empirical evidence that bodies exist, bodies do not exist. What one takes to be bodies are bundles of mental sensations and ideas, and their cause, Berkeley says, is God.

If one adds to Berkeley's reasoning the Cartesian conclusion that one is conscious only in the present moment only of one's own sensations and ideas, it is an easy step to the solipsism of the present moment. Berkeley does not take this step. Instead, he infers the existence of minds other than his own by analogy. And he posits the existence of God as the creator of finite minds and of a persisting world of sensations and ideas. God sets finite minds the task of figuring out which sensations and ideas are the causes of which other sensations and ideas, and gives finite minds the power to cause some of those sensations and ideas. Why does God do this? Berkeley does not say, but given that Berkeley was a Bishop and a good Christian, I speculate that he believed that God was testing each finite mind to see whether or not it is worthy of going to Heaven. But that aside, my purpose here is to show the Berkeleyan origins of metaphysical idealism, the view that reality is mental and that what one common-sensically takes to be material things are constructs out of sensations and ideas.

But to set the stage: Western philosophy has been dominated by giants of conceptual analysis. In Ancient philosophy, Plato and Aristotle organized human knowledge in frameworks of categories and arguments. Descartes did this in the Modern period, and in the eighteenth century, Kant isolated and organized the categories of understanding. Analysis on this level was also done for mathematics by Euclid, who is not generally classified as a philosopher but as a mathematician, and later it was pursued by Saint Augustine—who first proposed the *cogito*—who is generally classified as a philosopher of religion.

In contemporary philosophy—since the eighteenth century—the giant of categorical analysis is Immanuel Kant, whose structuring of human thought and knowledge I discuss in the previous chapter. Idealism, as framed by Kant, was dominant in Western philosophy from Kant to Bertrand Russell and G. E. Moore. Russell attacked Idealism implicitly and explicitly in *Problems of Philosophy* (1912) and in his pioneering attempt to construct the material world out of sense-data, *Our Knowledge of the External World* (1914). Moore made a famous attack on Idealism in his "Proof of the External World" (1932). But the Idealism that flowered after the publication of Kant's *Critique of Pure Reason* was never defeated outright. At least in Anglo-American philosophy, Idealism simply fizzled out after the deaths of such major figures as Josiah Royce at Harvard in 1916 and John McTaggart at Cambridge in 1925. In the 1930s, it was discarded as nonsense by advocates of the scientifically based philosophy of logical positivism, and of the language-analysis philosophy of Ludwig Wittgenstein. Certainly at major universities there were graduate seminars on Kant and Hegel—I took a famous one on Kant at the University of Michigan taught by Paul Henle—but that was about it. I convey here a major-university disdain for, and ignorance of, the programs at religiously oriented philosophy departments in smaller institutions. A twentieth-century Idealist I do not consider here is the philosopher of religion, Charles Hartshorne.

Why did Idealism bomb? Kant's deduction of the categories, and his outline of human thought deserves its place along with the conceptual analyses of Plato, Aristotle, and even with that of Euclid. Kant's logical analyses stand. On the other hand, the metaphysics of Idealism is totally unsupported. I have been very careful in my discussion of Kant above to make clear that Kant himself was completely aware that his logical constructions were only hypothetical, and that he does not conceal this fact from his readers. He points out that he has no proof that a world in space and time actually exists that manifests the categories of understanding he describes. His is one of the greatest analyses, perhaps the greatest, of the structure of human thought, but there is no proof that it describes an actually existing world.

Is there a way to overcome this ignorance of the existence of an existing world to which the categories apply? Yes. Faith. Trust in God.

The scientifically, empirically oriented Logical Positivists, bolstered in the 1930s by the advancement of science, an advance culminated by the splitting of the atom, Positivists viewed believers in a supernatural, incomprehensible God Who created the world out of nothing, with disdain, pity, and at bottom baffled amazement.

The flavor, the foundation of this religious idealism is best expressed by Josiah Royce, who was one of the last of the great assured and prolific of the religious idealists. In his *The World and the Individual, Gifford Lectures, Second Series, Nature, Man, and the Moral Order, Lecture VI, The Human Self*, Royce summarizes his position as follows:

> Our Idealism has depended, from the first, upon the thesis that the Internal and External meaning of any finite process of experience are dependent each upon the other, so that if the whole meaning and intent of any finite

instant of life is fully developed, and perfectly embodied, this Whole Meaning of the instant becomes identical with the Universe, with the Absolute, with the life of God. Even now, whatever you are or seek, the implied whole meaning of even your blindest striving is identical with the entire expression of the divine Will. And it is in this aspect of the world that we have found the unity of Being. (pp. 270–71)

I wonder how many philosophy students in the Anglo-American world today have read Royce. I do know what most of them—and most of the readers of this book—would make of the above passage. They would ask: What on earth is this man Royce talking about? And granting that one gets the sense of what is he saying, how on earth does he know all those things? But I do not include the passage just to make a smart remark. Royce continues:

In its knowledge of Being, the independent Self of any theoretical form of Realism, when once the independence of the individual Self has come to be recognized, tends to become in extreme cases, solipsistic. (p. 283)

You indeed know, although never in a merely direct way, *that* you exist. But in the present life you never find out, in terms of any direct experience, *what* you are. I know that I am, as this individual human Self, only in so far as every Internal Meaning, that of my present experience included, sends me elsewhere, or to some Other, for its complete interpretation, while this particular sort of Internal Meaning, such as gets expressed in the Cartesian *cogito ergo sum*, the meaning whereby I come to be aware of myself as this individual different from the rest of the world, implies and demands, for its complete embodiment, some sort of contrast between Self and not-Self. (p. 287)

Royce was the most distinguished, and most self-confident, Harvard philosopher of his day, his immediate competition consisting of three of the greatest of American philosophers: William James, Charles Sanders Peirce, and George Santayana. Not one of them was a threat to Royce's claim to esoteric knowledge about God, spirit, and the constitution of the human self and the universe. That is, William James said that if one's belief has no pragmatic or empirical implications, one is free to believe it. Santayana was a poet. And the logician Peirce was a very difficult person who did not have a professorship.

Of the four, Royce is virtually unknown to contemporary Anglo-American philosophers today. The reason is that practically none of them could or would have any idea what Royce is talking about. Kant's categorical analyses of concepts make sense. But how does Royce know that

> the Internal and External meaning of my finite process of experience are dependent each upon the other, so that if the whole meaning and intent of any finite instant of life is fully developed, and perfectly embodied, this Whole Meaning of the instant becomes identical with the Universe, with the Absolute, with the life of God. (pp. 270–71)

How does Royce know the Universe, the Absolute, and the life of God?

I make some effort to survey the views of some of the major idealist philosophers below. My primary question is the same for them all: How do they know the things they claim to know about the self, the world, the existence and the nature of God or the Absolute? In particular, why and how they believe they know what they claim about the Absolute baffles me. Obviously this is in some part because my training in graduate school was by Robert G. Turnbull (who was the first Ph.D. of the pioneer of philosophical analysis, Wilfrid Sellars), Gustav Bergmann (who was the youngest member of the Vienna Circle of logical positivists), and the preeminent scholar of skepticism, Richard H. Popkin with whom I wrote my Ph.D. thesis. Why do I flaunt those names? In part, to explain to myself my interest in the odd, neglected corners of philosophy. But also it is to explain to you, the reader, why Idealism baffles me.

To this end, here are some long (but I need them to make my point) passages from one of the best known Idealists, John

McTaggart Ellis McTaggart (1866–1925) from his *The Nature of Existence* (1921):

433. We have come to the conclusion that all that exists is spiritual, that the primary parts in the system of determining correspondence are selves, and that the secondary parts of all grades are perceptions. The selves, then, occupy an important position in the universe. They, and they alone, are primary parts. And they, and they alone, are percipients. This distinguishes them from their own parts, which are all secondary parts in the system of determining correspondence, and which are perceptions and not percipients.

We have now to consider what further conclusions as to selves and as to determining correspondence, can be deduced from these results. And, in the first place, is it true, not only, as we have just said, that all primary parts are selves, but also that all selves are primary parts?

This also must be the case. For the primary parts form a set of parts of the universe, and they contain between them all the content of the universe. If there were any other selves, then the content of each would have to fall within one or more primary parts which are selves. In that case one self would include another, or two selves would have a part in common. But we came to the conclusion in Chapter xxxvi that this is impossible.

434. Since all selves are primary parts, it follows that I myself, and any selves whom, in present experience, I know empirically, are primary parts. . . .

A . . . consequence which follows from the fact that all selves are primary parts is that the universe cannot be a self. The universe cannot be a primary part, for it is either a primary whole or a group of primary wholes. Moreover

the universe contains primary parts, and therefore contains selves; and no self can be a part of another self.

A third consequence which follows from this fact is that
Solipsism must be false. Solipsism is the belief that no substance exists except the person who is holding that belief,
and the parts of that person. But the universe must contain
more than one primary part, and since the solipsist is a
self, he is a primary part, and there are one or more primary parts outside him. (footnote 1. Of course this leaves
it possible that the universe should consist only of the
solipsist and one other self, but then [if this were the case]
the solipsist is mistaken in his solipsism.) (McTaggert, *The
Nature of Experience*, Vol. 2, pp. 120–21)

I give these long quotations to illustrate what baffles me: *How does
McTaggart know all this?* And what he is talking about? And how
did he come to his conclusions about what he is talking about? So
much the worse for me? I explain my position below.
McTaggart is aware that Idealism is in danger of leading to solipsism,
and his purported refutation of solipsism consists in stating with no
argument (or at least none I can discern) that the universe consists at
least "of the [purported] solipsist and one other self."
McTaggart continues his discussion of solipsism by considering what
he presents as the view of solipsism of Francis Herbert Bradley
(1846–1924) in Bradley's *Appearance and Reality*. McTaggart says
that in Bradley's *Appearance and Reality*:

> **435.** [Bradley's] argument rests on the contention that the
> self "involves and only exists through an intellectual con-
> struction. The self is thus a construction based on, and
> itself transcending, immediate experience." (fn. 2.
> *Appearance and Reality*, ch. xxvii, p. 524, 2nd ed.)

> Thus . . . it is unjustifiable to base the possibility of solip-
> sism on the ground that I am more certain of the existence
> of myself than of the existence of anything outside myself.
> My self and the external world have each to be reached by

inference. . . . If that inference does not give me justification for believing in something existent outside myself, it
does not give me justification for believing in myself. . . .
[But] the solipsist, who does not accept the existence of
anything outside himself, has to introduce into his explanation unconscious states of mind, and states of mind
which occurred in the past . . . of which the mind is not
conscious . . . [which are] not, of course, perceived. Nor
are past states of mind perceived in the present. Thus the
solipsist has to assert the existence of substances which he
does not perceive, just as much as the believer in external
existence does. And so it is still the case that he has to trust
to inference for his belief in substances. . . . [Finally, i]f
the sensa, or whatever appear as sensa, are not parts of the
percipient self—and this seems much the most probable
view—then solipsism is clearly false, since those things
which I perceive as sensa do unquestionably exist.
(McTaggart, Vol. II, pp. 121–23)

McTaggart concludes by concurring with Bradley that

the solipsist has to accept the existence which he does not
perceive [and that] those things which I perceive as sensa
do unquestionably exist [independently of being per-
ceived]. (p. 122)

If the sensa, or whatever appear as sensa, are not parts of
the percipient self—and this seems much the most probable view—then solipsism is clearly false, since those things
which I perceive as sensa do unquestionably exist. (p. 123)

These passages show that McTaggart does not recognize, or refuses
to accept, that the implication of the *cogito ergo sum*—solipsism of
the present moment—assures the existence only of the sensations and
ideas that one is conscious of in the present moment. Such momentary consciousness does *not* even imply, let alone assure, the existence
of a consciousness or self that persists in existence through time, nor
of past states of mind, or unperceived sensa.

Explicitly, solipsism of the present moment neither implies or proves the existence of anything but the sensations and ideas one is conscious of in the present moment. Nothing that persists through time is implied or proved. All that exists for the solipsist of the present moment is one burst of consciousness in that present moment. Nothing requires the solipsist to accept the existence of bodies or causes that persist through time, nor even the existence of time itself. There is no reason why the present moment of consciousness, uncaused, is not all that exists.

This is why, as I discuss below, the Absolute is presented as timeless, and as perceiving in one burst of cosmic consciousness, all that all finite selves experience in temporal sequence.

F. C. S. Schiller, however, spells out these present-moment solipsistic implications of idealism in his article "Is Absolute Idealism Solipsistic?" published in *The Journal of Philosophy, Psychology, and Scientific Methods* in 1906. Schiller says that solipsism is usually defectively defined

> as the doctrine that *as all experience is my experience, I alone exist*, it is taken for granted (1) that there can be only one solipsist and (2) that he must be 'I' and not 'you.'

He goes on to say:

> Solipsism . . . should be conceived with greater generality [to] cover the doctrine that the whole of reality has a single owner and is relative to a single experient, and that beyond such an experient nothing further need be assumed, without implying that I am the only 'I' that owns the universe. *Any 'I' will do.* Any I that thinks it is all that is, is a solipsist. And solipsism will be true if *any one* of the many 'I's' that there are, or may be, solipsists is right and really is all that is. Provided, of course, he knows it. (p. 86)

To carry on his analysis, Schiller considers the absolute idealist notion that

> my (our) experience . . . in all its forms . . . seems to rest essentially on an argument from the ideality of my (our)

experience to the ideality of all experience. For the former is taken as proof that all reality is relative to a knower, who, however, is not necessarily the individual knower, but may (or must) be an all-embracing subject, sustaining us and all the world besides. (p. 86)

Schiller concludes that this "is equivalent to saying (1) that *the absolute must be a solipsist*, and (2) that *solipsism is the absolute truth*" and that "the inference from absolute idealism to solipsism seems unavoidable" (pp. 87–88).

Instead of being absorbed in the absolute . . . each individual solipsist would swallow up the absolute. . . . The absolute *ex hypothesi* is and owns each 'private self.' And the absolute is a solipsist. This feature, therefore, of the truth must be reflected in each private self. They must all be solipsists. But this is merely the truth of solipsism looked at from the standpoint of the private self. (p. 88)

The result of this tortured reasoning is not what an idealist might desire, or expect.

It now turns out that the absolute itself insists on the truth of solipsism. And yet if solipsism is true, there is no reason at all for transcending the individual experience of each solipsist! It would seem, therefore, that we can not admit the truth of solipsism without ruining our absolute, nor admit our absolute without admitting the truth of solipsism. (p. 89)

The final point of Schiller's argument that the absolute is solipsistic is thus not directed against solipsism as such, but against absolute idealism.

J. G. Fichte in his *Science of Knowledge* (1794) comes to conclusions apparently similar to those of Bradley, although I do not claim to understand very well (if at all) what Fichte says:

The source of all reality is the self, for this is what is immediately and absolutely posited. . . . But the self *exists* because it *posits itself*, and it posits itself because it exists.

52

Hence, self-positing and existence are one and the same.
Hence, all reality is active. (p. 129)

It seems to me that this supports solipsism, given that one—the self—
has grounds for positing only one's own existence.

* * *

What is absolute idealism? It has to do with the Absolute. In all
my training in philosophy, and in my long career as a professor of
philosophy, I have never until now had to consider just what the
Absolute is. Josiah Royce explains the Absolute in his *The World and
the Individual* (1901):

> Our idealism has depended, from the first, upon the the-
> sis that the Internal and External meanings of any finite
> process of experience are dependent each upon the other,
> so that if the whole meaning and intent of any finite
> instant of life is fully developed, and perfectly embodied,
> this Whole Meaning of the instant becomes identical with
> the Universe, with the Absolute, with the life of God.
> Even now, whatever you are or seek, the implied whole
> meaning of even your blindest striving is identical with
> the entire expression of the divine Will. And it is in this
> aspect of the world that we have found the unity of Being.
> (pp. 270–71)

My basic question above remains: How do Royce (and other
Absolute Idealists) know all this? The Whole Meaning, the Universe,
the Absolute, the life of God, the divine Will, the unity of Being?

Absolute Idealism appears to make perfect sense at least to some
philosophers who believe in God. God created everything, controls
everything, is ineffable, and needs no proof.

Doesn't this "unity of Being" imply solipsism? Yes, for Realism:

> In its knowledge of Being, the independent Self of any the-
> oretical form of Realism when once the independence of
> the individual Self has come to be recognized, tends to
> become in extreme cases, solipsistic. (p. 283)

But for Absolutism:

From our point of view, your distinction from the rest of the universe, your contrast with other selves, your uniqueness, your freedom, your individuality, all depend upon one essential principle. This world that we live in is, in its wholeness, the expression of one determinate and absolute purpose, the fulfillment of divine will. According to our account, every new Self that arises in time must find its place *within* the life of a larger and inclusive Selfhood. (pp. 292–93)

Is this "larger and inclusive Selfhood" the Absolute? Is this Absolute a solipsist?

In his massive study *The Idealistic Argument in Recent British and American Philosophy* (1933), G. Watts Cunningham (to whom I am greatly indebted) presents the argument of the personal idealist, George Holmes Howison (1834–1916), that the Absolute Idealism of Royce leads to solipsism:

If the Infinite Self *includes* us all, and all our experiences . . . in the unity of one life, and includes us and them *directly*; if there is but one and the same final Self for us each and all; then, with a literalness indeed appalling, He is we, and we are He; nay, He is I, and I am He. . . . Is not He the sole *agent*? Are we anything but the steadfast and changeless modes of His eternal thinking and perceiving? Or, if we read the conception in the second way, what becomes of *Him*? Then, surely, He is but another name for *me*. (Cunningham, p. 303, from Howison's comments on Royce's comments in *The Conception of God*, p. 84)

Is the Absolute a solipsist, or, on the other hand, is the solipsist the Absolute? Idealists take it for granted that the Absolute is the source of the sensations and ideas everyone has. They assume that it is impossible for a solipsist to cause the sensations and ideas he has in the present moment. This is on the assumption that these sensations and ideas need a cause. But for the solipsist, they just appear in the present moment. This seems bothersome or worrisome only to those—such as the Idealists—who have apparently accepted, without any grounds or proof, the common-sense notion that everything must or does have a cause.

In his *Appearance and Reality* (1893), Chapter XXI, Solipsism, F. H. Bradley asks:

> Have we any reason to believe in the existence of anything beyond our private selves? . . . The argument in favor of Solipsism, put most simply, is as follows. 'I cannot transcend experience, and experience must be *my* experience. From this it follows that nothing beyond my self exists; for what is experience in its [my self's] states?' (p. 218)

Then Bradley goes on to state precisely the doctrine of solipsism of the present moment, and to reject the reduction of the solipsist's existence to the present moment as absurd:

> My self, as an existence to which phenomena belong as its adjectives, is supposed to be given by direct experience. But this gift plainly is an illusion. Such an experience can supply us with *no reality beyond that of the moment. There is no faculty which can deliver the immediate revelation of a self beyond the present.* And so, if Solipsism finds its one real thing in experience, that thing is confined to the limits of the mere 'this'. *But with such a reflection we have already, so far, destroyed Solipsism as positive, and as anything more than a sufficient reason for total skepticism. . . . Direct experience is unable to transcend the mere 'this'. . . . [W]e are . . . not supplied with the self upon which Solipsism is founded.* [my italics] (p. 219)

Bradley recognizes and states the conditions that lead to solipsism of the present moment, but because he assumes without argument that solipsism is not true, he dismisses this argument, the conditions of which he admits. Solipsism of the present moment reduces the self to consciousness in the present moment. Bradley assumes that the self abides through time, conscious of passing moments.

"If Solipsism is to be proved," Bradley says "it must transcend direct experience" (p. 221).

This requires the assumption that a world exists beyond the

sensations and ideas the solipsist experiences in the present moment. But Cartesian solipsism, based on what one consciously knows for certain to exist—which is what one is aware of in the present moment—does not require transcending the direct experience of the present moment.

Bradley goes on to say, "It is both possible and necessary to transcend what is given at large. Our private self is not a resting-place which logic can justify" (p. 221). But he does not attempt to show that there is no possibility that the immediate sensory given may be all there is. He sets up, but does not undertake, the project of deriving a public world external to immediate consciousness from private immediate, momentary sensory data. This project is a construction job—later undertaken by Carnap and Goodman—to show how a public world can be derived out of or generated from private, momentary sensory data.

Bradley poses two crucial questions:

> Has a man a right to say that something exists, beside that which at this moment he actually feels? And is it possible, on the other side, to identify reality with the immediate present? (p. 221)

He simply states without argument that

> the attempt to remain within the boundary of the mere 'this' [present moment] is hopeless. . . . To remain within the presented is neither defensible nor possible. We are compelled alike by necessity and by logic to transcend it. (pp. 221–22)

Bradley thus shows that he understands the crucial, critical aspect of solipsism of the present moment. Bradley appeals to one's sense of passing time, which he takes to be really happening. But the thesis of solipsism of the present moment is that despite this sense of one's being conscious during a sequence of specious presences, one is not and cannot be an entity experiencing actual passing time. One has evidence that one exists only in the present moment of consciousness, which is now. Now is always the present moment, or conversely, the present moment is always now. And at this present moment one is always conscious of memory ideas of purported past moments, which one has no evidence ever existed.

To put it precisely, the present moment is the temporal point when one is conscious of existing *only at that point of present time.* One is conscious of *no movement from past temporal point to present temporal point. Whenever one considers it, one is always at the present moment.* The sense of this passage through time is an illusion. It seems as though one has moved from point to point in time because in the present moment one has purported (false) memory ideas of purported past moments (that one has no proof ever existed). But in fact, one is conscious only in and of the *present* moment in time.

This is the crucial point, as Bradley clearly sees. He says that

> if you have a right to believe in a self beyond the present [that is, a right to believe that you are a self that persists through time, which right you do not have], you have the same right to maintain also the existence of other selves [so you do not have the right to believe in the existence of other selves]. (p. 224)

Bradley continues that "It is by the same kind of argument that we reach our own past and future" (Bradley, p. 225). And he says that "we can go to foreign selves by a process no worse [note that he recognizes that his argument is inadequate] than the *construction* [my italics] which establishes our own self" (p. 227).

After having read a number of other idealists, I have only admiration for Bradley's comprehension of solipsism of the present moment, and for his recognition of the fact that his arguments do not defeat it:

> I cannot *prove* that yesterday's self, which I construct, did, as such, have an actual existence in the past. . . . Both other selves and my own self are intellectual constructions. . . . But . . . neither is demonstrable. . . . [W]e can go to foreign selves by a process no worse than the construction which establishes our own self. . . . Even if I had secured a right to the possession of my past self, and no right to the acceptance of other selves as real.

. . . It is true that all I experience is my state—so far as I experience it. Even the Absolute, is my reality, is my state of mind. . . . (pp. 226–28)

But where does that leave us, or rather, where does it leave Bradley? In his final chapter, XXVII, Ultimate Doubts, he summarizes his reasoning for coming to the following conclusion:

Beyond all doubt then it is clear that Reality is one. It has unity but we must go on to ask, a unity of what? And we have already found that all we know consists wholly of experience. Reality must be, therefore, one Experience, and to doubt this conclusion is impossible.

We can discover nothing that is not either feeling or thought or will or emotion or something else of the kind. [Obviously, then] [i]t may be objected that, if Reality is proved one experience, Solipsism follows. (pp. 463–64)

Does Bradley escape this result? No, and again he is honest enough to make that clear. He also makes clear that he understands that the solipsist of the present moment is confined to contents of his consciousness at the moment. And thus a self persisting through time must be constructed:

Perhaps in all cases the self—and at any rate always the soul—involves and only exists through an intellectual construction. The self is thus a construction based on, and itself transcending immediate experience [i.e., experience confined to the present moment]. (pp. 464–65)

What Bradley is working toward is the Idealist conclusion that

Everything, myself included, is essential to, and is inseparable from, the Absolute. . . . [I]t is only in feeling that I can directly encounter Reality. . . . The world and experience are, taken at large, the same. And my experience and its states, in a sense, actually are the whole world; for to this slight extent the one reality is actually my self. (p. 466)

Bradley comes to a final conclusion that is literally that of the solipsist of the present moment: "Reality is one, and is a single experience" (p. 473). The question that then arises—or remains—is: Is the Absolute a solipsist of the present moment?

In his massive study *James and Bradley: American Truth and British Reality* (1993), T. L. S. Sprigge presents Bradley's Absolute in such a way that the answer is yes. Sprigge concludes that for Bradley:

(1) The Absolute or totality of all things is not a mere aggregate or assemblage of things—it is much more truly one than many. . . .

(2) The Absolute is a timeless experience or state of mind inconceivably rich in the elements which go to make it up but still having something like the kind of unity which belongs to *a human person's experience as it occurs at any moment*. [my italics] It contains every conscious experience which any conscious person has had or will have, and thereby contains everything, since, for Bradley, there is nothing except experience. Just as what a human hears, feels, sees, thinks, etc. at any one moment is fairly multiple, yet makes up a single experience, so does every ingredient of the world go to make up this single vast cosmic experience which is the Absolute, or the Universe as it really is.

(3) The Absolute is not a person. A person must feel itself in contrast to a world, which provides its environment, whereas the Absolute experiences everything as an element in its own being.

(4) Although the Absolute is the *All*, there is a sense in which the *All* or *Whole* is present in each of its *parts* or *aspects*. As a first suggestion of what this means one might say that it is present in all its parts somewhat as someone's personality may be present in all his acts, or in which the

total character of a work of art permeates all its elements. (Sprigge, p. 265)

Sprigge calls this "Bradley's panexperientialist metaphysic."

> Thus the Absolute is a single experience in which everything is contained in timelessly. Everything which is there really is either an experience or an element in an experience. . . . [T]he conception of [Bradley's] Absolute is modeled on a conception of our single states of consciousness, as they occur moment by moment. (Sprigge, pp. 275–76)

And on p. 493, Sprigge refers to Bradley's metaphysics as "the philosophy of the present." And Sprigge concludes that

> for Bradley . . . there is ultimately just the eternal Absolute which contains all experience, that is, all there is . . . all moments of time are just eternally there. (p. 577)

Sprigge himself defends Absolute Idealism in *The Vindication of Absolute Idealism* (1983), in which, like Bradley, he presents the Absolute as a solipsist of the present moment. Note that Sprigge himself never says that the Absolute is a solipsist of the present moment. But this inference is inevitable from what he does say:

> The universe, in its true being, is a system of centers of experieince in holistic relations to one another within it, which make it, or depend on its being . . . a concrete whole at least as genuinely individual as anything within it. Our only familiar examples of really concrete wholes, consisting of elements in holistic relations one to another, are momentary centers of experience. The universe, or Absolute . . . somehow stands to the various momentary centres in it as they do to their contents. . . . We must conceive [the Absolute] as some kind of whole with contrasts within it between earlier and later phases, as well as of phases which go together as more fully 'at once', so that it is a kind of specious present, but as something which is

60

non-temporal in as much as it neither is, nor feels itself to be, a phase in a temporal process. (p. 251)

I present these descriptions of the Absolute, Bradley's and Sprigge's derived from Bradley, in full without giving any explanatory exposition of them because I do not know how to make sense of such claims as that of "contrasts . . . between earlier and later phases as well as phases which go together as fully 'at once', so that it [the Absolute] is a kind of specious present."

I do believe, however, that I have sufficiently shown that the Idealists such as Bradley and Sprigge support my claim that solipsism of the present moment is empirically supported, but also that the Absolute is a, or if you will, the, solipsist of the present moment.

J. G. Fichte in his *Science of Knowledge* (1794) comes to conclusions apparently similar to those of Bradley, although I do not claim to understand very well (if at all) what Fichte says:

> The source of all reality is the self, for this is what is immediately and absolutely posited. . . . But the self *exists* because it *posits itself*, and it posits itself because it exists. Hence, self-positing and existence are one and the same. Hence, all reality is active. (p. 129)

I find perfectly understandable—even to the demands of contemporary empirical philosophical analysis or positivism—the argument for solipsism of the present moment that derives from Descartes's *cogito ergo sum*, that one knows for certain that one exists only when one is thinking, and that one knows one is thinking only in the present moment. The grounds, however, on which Idealists argue for the existence of the Absolute as the single atemporal consciousness of all the temporal thoughts of all finite consciousnesses are incoherent.

Personal Identity

Solipsism has been addressed in discussions about the nature of one's personal identity. A classic paper on this subject is "Personal Identity" by Derek Parfit (1971), which has given rise to hundreds of articles and many books. They are addressed to the question of what binds the thoughts, sensations, ideas, impressions of a given person together in space and over time. It is taken for granted that one has a body that persists through time, and that associated with this body is a conscious mind that experiences and remembers sensations and ideas that one has through time. One's self is usually presented as something that is different from one's body, and that one's personal identity is derived from the conscious sensations and ideas this self has through time. Generally speaking, these sensations and ideas are caused by one's bodily interactions with the material world, interactions as simple as bumping into bodies and as complex as interpreting written and spoken words.

Then questions are posed, such as whether or not a set of memories or a consciousness can be divided or duplicated.

I do not delve into this vast and convoluted literature on personal identity because I argue against the unsupported and usually unexamined ontological claim on which it is based: that there is a human body or brain that exists through time. As I argue above, my thesis is that there is no direct empirical evidence for the existence of a human body or brain, let alone one that exists through time. More than that, there is no direct empirical evidence for the existence of time. On empirical grounds, all that is known for certain to exist is one's sensations and ideas in the present moment, some of which have an aura of representing sensations and ideas one has had in the past. But all these representations exist only at the moment one has them. The unintelligible notion that a stretch of time exists, with the implication that moments of past time still exist now, is derived from the impressions of memories that occur at the present moment but appear to represent sensations and ideas that existed in the past. One's sensations and ideas that have a sense of representing past sensations and ideas exist in fact only now; the only existence is one's present sensations and ideas now; there is no evidence for the existence of anything other than one's present sensations and ideas now.

Because of the fact that one's being always exists in the present moment and only in the present moment, to speak of one's mind is to speak simply and only of one's present sensations and ideas. In opposition to Descartes and his followers, there is no mind or body that has or experiences those sensations and ideas. Nothing exists except one's sensations and ideas in the present moment.

The fact is that the entire literature on personal identity exemplified by that associated with Derek Parfit's article on the subject is based on the assumption that the problem I am investigating is solved. It is based on the assumption that one can actually know that other minds than one's own exist. But solipsism is a view of the universe based on the realization that all one can know for certain to exist are the sensations and ideas one is experiencing at the present moment. There is no immediately perceived evidence that any other minds than one's own exist. There is no directly perceived evidence even that there is such a thing as a mind, let alone such a thing as a body, that persists through time. Nor is there any immediate empirical evidence that one's own consciousness is a function of either a material brain that exists in space or a mental mind that persists through time. One certainly has the impression that one has a conscious mind that persists through time as a passenger in a material body that persists in space and through time. But this impression is an illusion.

Nor is there any empirical evidence that any consciousness exists except one's own.

Note well that my entire argument for solipsism rests on this principle: certain knowledge obtains solely in immediate perception, of what one perceives to exist in the present moment. All conclusions based on any other foundation are hypothetical and uncertain. They all depend on memory, which I argue is an illusion.

Parfit *et al.* assume that a conscious human being is an entity consisting of a mind conjoined with a body that exists in space and persists through time. Moreover, the vast majority of twenty-first-century neuroscientists and philosophers of mind assume that one's conscious mind is the brain. This brain is not the Cartesian or nineteenth-century material brain, but rather it is the neurophysiological nervous system extending throughout one's body consisting at bottom (so far as is known at present) of sub-atomic particles and forces. It is this entity that is assumed to persist through time. This neurophysiological system is taken to be continuously active in response to its interactions with the material world outside one's body.

The theory of this neurophysiological system is a fabulous construction of the human intellect. But there is no direct empirical evidence that such a system exists. In a practical context, it is useful for working with bodies (which also are intellectual constructions), just as is the law of falling bodies.

In this scientific context, the opposition to my argument for solipsism is that *no* scientific theory is certain. Science is entirely hypothetical. It is pragmatic. If a theory works, it is accepted. If a theory does not work, it is rejected. What more does one want or need?

I understand this objection, but solipsism is not a scientific theory. It is an ontological theory based on the certain truth that while one is conscious of thinking, one exists.

Solipsism is a position that derives epistemologically from answering the question: what can one be absolutely certain exists? The answer is that one can be absolutely certain of the existence of the sensations and ideas one is having at the present moment—a direct report of immediately present conscious experience. The ground on which solipsism based is the immediate empirical fact that the only entities in the universe that one knows certainly to exist are one's present sensations and ideas.

It is often argued that it is absurd to demand such certainty. No, it is not absurd. But is confining. It changes nothing about how one common-sensically experiences and scientifically thinks about the world. But it can alter what one believes oneself and the world to be.

My concern here is neither practical nor scientific, but rather it is epistemological and metaphysical. First, it is about what one can know for certain. Then, it is about what can be known for certain actually to exist. At least since the advent of Logical Positivism in the

1930s, most Anglo-American philosophers have accepted the positivistic view that nothing about the empirical world can be known with absolute certainty. Related to this view is the claim that metaphysics—any assertion about what really exists in the universe—is nonsense. Positivists claim that metaphysics is nonsense because no empirical conclusions can either confirm nor disconfirm the truth of a metaphysical system.

But solipsism taken to be a metaphysical system is confirmed by a factual empirical report about what one knows to exist for certain at the present moment.

I base my argument for solipsism on the empirical facts about human consciousness and perception. Far from denying as positivists do that certain knowledge is impossible about the world human beings inhabit, I base my conclusions on the certain knowledge one can and does have about one's conscious experience of the sensations and ideas that populate a human being's world.

The positivists' conclusion that solipsism is nonsense because it is a metaphysics, is one reason why the empirical evidence for solipsism has been ignored, denied, and fobbed off with jokes. But the major reason why solipsism has been put aside is the claim that no one does or could believe it. Or, if anyone were crazy enough to believe it, it would make no difference to that person's life. Or if a lot of people believed it, it would make no difference to their ordinary experience and ordinary lives even if it were true. None of those results are obvious. And of course those that imply or depend on the existence of more than one consciousness, or on the view that consciousness persists through time, are based on not understanding the thesis of solipsism of the present moment.

I argue that solipsism of the present moment is true on the basis of the detailed exposition given of it here. I also contend that belief in solipsism need not or might not make any difference to the way the solipsist lives his life.

Could there be more than one solipsist? Why not? The condition or predicament of being confined to certain knowledge only of one's own immediate sensations and ideas does not necessarily imply that one is the only conscious being in the universe. It implies only that one is confined to consciousness of sensations and ideas of which only he can be conscious. This experience provides no certain knowledge that there are other conscious beings in the universe than oneself. This is a lonely position.

If solipsism is true, and if it were recognized to be so, this knowledge could have an enormous effect on whoever is aware of its truth. One response may actually be the virtually hysterical refusal of positivists (see succeeding chapters) to admit the solid evidence for solipsism, or, when this evidence cannot be avoided, to refuse to take solipsism seriously.

The sense-data foundations of logical positivism—as I show in succeeding chapters—lead to solipsism. In my experience, the most common reaction to this conclusion by most people who understand it is a shrug of the shoulders. This reaction is not necessarily inappropriate. After all, even if solipsism is true, one's life experience is not altered.

If solipsism is true—and the evidence for its truth is overwhelming—why is it ignored or simply set aside with jokes? I do not think there is any conspiracy to ignore it. I think that one reason an inquiry like the present one has not been undertaken is simply because of the (perhaps suppressed) belief that if solipsism is true, there is nothing one can do about it.

If solipsism is true, this truth changes nothing about how one common-sensically or scientifically experiences and thinks about the world. But it might alter one's ultimate meditations about the world and oneself.

Before continuing with my defense of solipsism, I present here a typical rejection of it. This is from *The Problems of Perception* by R. J. Hirst in a classic defense of the representative theory of perception. He argues that privately experienced sensations and ideas are representative of public material bodies in the world external to one's mind:

> To show that the Representative Theory gives the best explanation of these correlations of [sense-]data (granted *pace* common-sense that they are private data), we must compare it with rivals. One of these is solipsism, the view that only one's own stream of ideas or sensations exists. This has the basic weakness that the only reason anyone could have for rejecting the almost irresistible

common-sense assumption that we are aware of other persons and public objects is that the evidence of physiology and hallucinations shows that such awareness is really only of sensations; but such evidence rests almost entirely on the evidence of other people, e.g., of neurologists or, in the case of the more spectacular hallucinations, those who have had the experience. Furthermore the sequence of experiences involved in what would ordinarily be described as being given information by another person and then verifying it for oneself is not easy to explain on solipsistic lines; one would have to suppose that one only dreamt or imagined that there was another person, and this would amount to denying the distinction between dreaming (or imagining) and reality, with the resultant difficulty of explaining away the tests and differences on which the distinction is normally based (e.g. the continuity of causal law between two waking states but not between two dream states). In fact, of course, no one believes solipsism is satisfactory, and philosophers would not give it a moment's thought were it not for the difficulty of conclusively refuting it, as opposed to showing that it is not plausible. (pp. 161–62)

First, Hirst concludes—as do so many people arguing against solipsism—that solipsism is "not plausible," without giving any precise definition of what he means by "plausible" at all.

What is obvious here is that this typical, and unusually detailed, rejection of solipsism exhibits clearly that it is not an argument at all. Hirst starts with admitting that there are private sense-data. This means that nobody can know what other people perceive, or whether or not they perceive anything at all. But then he appeals to the

almost [my italics] irresistible commonsense assumption that we are aware of other persons and public objects [for which] the evidence of physiology and hallucinations shows that such awareness is really only of sensations [and] such evidence rests *almost entirely on the evidence of other people* [my italics]. (p. 161)

Notice the two sentences qualified with "almost." This is a professional philosopher's devious way of qualifying a statement that is not certain with "almost" and then going on as though what is "almost" something or other is in fact certainly that something or other.

Then, as is typical in virtually all so-called refutations of solipsism, Hirst makes the assumption that there are other people. But even if he could prove that there are other people—and Hirst knows he cannot, or he would do it, because that proof in itself would destroy the arguments for solipsism—of what value would "the evidence of other people" be, given that one cannot examine their private sense-data to know what they perceive or even that they do perceive? Direct knowledge of other people's consciously perceived sensations and ideas would be required to determine whether or not their conscious perceptions and thoughts are like one's own. But if I did have direct knowledge of another person's perceptions, those perceptions would not belong to that other person, they would belong to me.

Hirst is similarly devious in talking about dreams. How do the sensations and ideas in dreams differ from those in waking life? The usual argument for their "unreality" is that what one perceives in dreams is not consistent in the way one takes perceptions one has when awake to be. But as perceptions and ideas, they are just as immediate and just as real as waking perceptions and ideas. Finally, his conclusion is classic:

> In fact, of course, *no one believes* solipsism is *satisfactory*, and philosophers would not give it a moment's thought were it not for the difficulty of *conclusively* refuting it, as opposed to showing that it is *not plausible*. (my italics, p. 162)

It is rather sad, and maybe even mean-spirited, to point out so bluntly how a philosopher weasels his way around problems that he cannot solve and that destroy the position he purports to be establishing—because the position he is opposing is "*not plausible*."

I know of no philosophical position in Western philosophy other than solipsism that has been so consistently and so cavalierly rejected on no grounds of intellectual argument at all. There may in fact be no other philosophical position that is rejected simply on the grounds that it is implausible or foolish or groundless. In fact, solipsism is neither implausible nor foolish nor groundless.

Hirst, however, is perfectly confident that he can dismiss solipsism just by saying (but not demonstrating) that solipsism is "not plausible." And despite the fact that there is "the difficulty of conclusively refuting it," he just leaves it there, and is confident that no one will challenge him to provide a conclusive refutation of such a silly position. He also is certain that anyone who does argue for solipsism will not be taken seriously. And that is taken to be the end of the matter.

What Hirst is avoiding is stating outright the fact that solipsism has not been refuted. I do not claim that it cannot possibly be refuted. I show that it has not been refuted.

First, of course, it is perfectly possible to believe in solipsism. And there is no contradiction if solipsists behave in the world like everyone else does. (Remember that the existence of more than one solipsist is not impossible.) But behaving as though there are other conscious people in the world does not mean that one believes there are other conscious people in the world, nor does it commit one to such a belief. Nor does such behavior either imply or prove that there are other conscious people in the world.

Behavior is in fact—as everyone who is not a fool knows—an unreliable indicator of what one believes. Just because one behaves as though there are other conscious beings in the universe proves nothing about what one believes about whether or not there are other conscious beings in the universe—and certainly such behavior is no proof that there are other conscious beings in the universe. In fact, the solipsist can go about his life seldom thinking about the fact that he is a solipsist.

Why not? Nothing concerning the fact that the solipsist is a solipsist need have any bearing whatsoever on his behavior. Why should it?

I am reminded of a bumper sticker I have long admired that I have been trying to find a place to insert in this exposition. It was a favorite of a very bright Ph.D. student of mine: You say I'm a bitch— is that a problem?

So if one says "I'm a solipsist," is that a problem?

I have remarked above how G. E. Moore, in his famous paper "Proof of an External World," which world includes other people, rejects solipsism by taking common-sense to be adequate for proving the existence of material bodies outside one's sensory images of them. And I described an exhibition for which he was famous, in which he holds up one hand and said "This is a hand," and then the other, and says that it also was a hand, and that is his proof of the existence of the ordinary world of common-sense bodies external to private sensory images and intellectual ideas.

First, let me say that Moore was not making a joke. No one would ever have accused Moore of joking.

"Ah," you say, "but in telling that story, are you not assuming the existence of the skylight as something external to the mind?"

Not at all. I'm just commenting on how a great philosopher did not take solipsism seriously, who believed that the way to refute it was not by argument, but simply by dismissing it by exhibiting bull-headed common sense.

Such frivolity is the end of the matter for all the philosophers in the Western tradition who revert to common-sense when their favorite theses provide no defense against a position such as solipsism that they cannot refute. They simply announce that it is "not plausible" and go merrily on their metaphysical way. I wonder if they are terrified, surely not by the prospect of solipsism itself, but by their inability to refute it.

Logical Positivism

In my youth, besides the metaphysical philosophies of the Continental Rationalists—Descartes, Leibniz, Spinoza—and the British Empiricists—Locke, Berkeley, Hume—I was raised on the constructivist philosophies of the Logical Positivists—A. J. Ayer, Rudolph Carnap, Nelson Goodman, and Gustav Bergmann. I now show that none of these philosophers escaped the solipsistic implications of basing human knowledge on the immediate data of the senses.

When one awakens into conscious existence, one becomes aware of what William James called "one great blooming, buzzing confusion." The Logical Positivists analyze this confusion into the data of the senses: touches, tastes, sounds, odors, and sights. Besides these basic five there are also feelings of fear and hope, etc., passions of love and hate, etc., and so on, a huge range of private, personal data that constitutes the immediate content of one's consciousness. The task such philosophers as Carnap and Goodman take upon themselves is to construct the public worlds of common-sense and of science out of this mélange of the private sense-data of myriad individuals. They never deny that the sense-data one perceives is immediate, private, and in itself unanalyzable. One can examine and separate elements in a sensory field (of sound, sight, etc.) but one cannot break down a color as seen into more basic elements. One might venture that an orange dot is a combination of red and yellow dots, but the red and yellow elements are not visible in the sensed orange dot itself, which is what it is and not another thing.

From elementary, minimum sense-data of multitudes of different types, a sense-datum philosopher's goal is to construct the complex worlds of common-sense and scientific objects as one knows them. This constructivism is the foundation of virtually all contemporary analytic philosophy, although few philosophers today begin at the sense-datum foundations. There is a very wide variety of such constructions, but virtually all of them falter at the seventeenth-century stumbling block—the distinction between mind and body.

Descartes's immaterial mind is self-conscious; his material body is not. So how can they interact, as they obviously do? As described above, Berkeley's way out of this conundrum is to deny that matter is a distinct substance, but rather is just a manifestation of the mental. Most contemporary Anglo-American philosophers and neuroscientists argue in turn that, on the contrary, the mind is a manifestation of the material brain.

Whatever brains are, there is no question but that consciousness arises from brain activity. The great goal of neuroscientists today is to show *how* consciousness arises out of the brain. The problem is that consciousness does not appear *as* brain activity. It seems to be on a different ontological plane from that of brain activity. In the seventeenth century, the question was: How can a material brain cause a mental idea? The twenty-first-century question is: How is consciousness generated by the material activity of the brain?

Of course today's notion of matter is very different from the seventeenth-century notion of matter, but today's conception of matter is just as alien to the conception of consciousness as was the seventeenth-century notion of matter. And we have no more notion of how matter causes consciousness than Descartes did in the seventeenth century.

The solipsist can argue that consciousness is not the problem. One has direct access to consciousness. What is hypothetical is the postulation of the material brain.

However it is brought about, one seems to have control of some of one's sensations and ideas. One can imagine all sorts of things (but not a square circle), and one can cause all sorts of events to happen, for example, the explosion of an atomic bomb. In a Berkeleyan world, think of the multitude of sensations one must cause oneself to have in a precise order to construct an atomic bomb. One certainly has the ability to cause oneself to have all those sensations. But if our world is one of Berkeleyan immaterialism, is not it odd, droll, puzzling, and amazing—that God so created the universe of mental things—of minds and the sensations and ideas minds have—such that a huge number of extremely complicated sensory experiences must be gone through before one can have the sensory experiences that follow from the explosion of an atomic bomb? Or, the sensations one must—and can—cause oneself to have to make and eat a peanut-butter sandwich?

God (according to Berkeley) put us here to learn what sensations follow one another to result in other sensations.

Passing strange.

Of course for the solipsist it is not surprising that the world of sensory experience and intellectual ideas is complex and weird. It differs from Berkeley's world only in being without any cause other than one's apparent (partial) ability to control some of the sensations and ideas one has.

A. J. Ayer (1910–1989)

The pioneering sense-datum philosopher, A. J. Ayer, constructs a world of public objects from private sense-data. In *Language, Truth and Logic*, Ayer dispenses with solipsism, not by denying any arguments for it, but by by-passing it:

> In thus combining a thoroughgoing phenomenalism with the admission that all sense-experiences, and the sense-contents which form part of them, are private to a single self, we are pursuing a course to which the following objection is likely to be raised. It will be said that anyone who maintains both that all empirical knowledge resolves itself on analysis into knowledge of the relationships of sense-contents, and also that the whole of a man's sense-history is private to himself, is logically obliged to be a solipsist—that is, to hold that no other people besides himself exist, or at any rate that there is no good reason to suppose that any other people beside himself exist. For it follows from his premises, so it will be argued, that the sense-experiences of another person cannot possibly form part of his own experience, and consequently that he cannot have the slightest ground for believing in their occurrence; and, in that case, if people are nothing but logical constructions out of their sense-experiences, he cannot have the slightest ground for believing in the existence of any other people. And it will be said that even if such a solipsistic doctrine cannot be shown to be self-contradictory, it is nevertheless known to be false. [Here Ayer cites L. S. Stebbing, *Logical Positivism and Analysis*.]

> I propose to meet this objection, not by denying that solipsism is known to be false, but by denying that it is a

necessary consequence of our epistemology. I am, indeed, prepared to admit that if the personality of others was something that I could not possibly observe, then I should have no reason to believe in the existence of anyone else. And in admitting this I am conceding a point which would not, I think, be conceded by the majority of those philosophers who hold, as we do, that a sense-content cannot belong to the sense-history of more than a single self. *They would maintain, on the contrary, that although one cannot in any sense observe the existence of other people, one can nevertheless infer their existence with a high degree of probability from one's own experiences.* [my italics.] They would say that my observation of a body whose behaviour resembled the behaviour of my own body entitled me to think it probable that that body was related to a self which I could not observe, in the same way as my body was related to my own observable self. (pp. 128–29)

Ayer says that one can infer the existence of other people "with a high degree of probability from one's own experiences" (p. 129). This is the typical bravado exhibited by all opponents of solipsism. No one has ever demonstrated what this probability amounts to or how it is determined. In fact, it is based on empty air.

The typical bravado argument against solipsism is exemplified by Ayer's justification for assuming the existence of other minds on the basis of the behavior of human bodies other than his own in the conclusion of his essay "On What There Is" in his *Philosophical Essays*:

This is a normal type of inductive argument; and I cannot see that it is in any degree invalidated by the fact that, however far one is able to extend the positive analogy, it always remains within the compass of one's own experience. (p. 214)

Of course one heroic way out of this inability to deny, or refute, the arguments for solipsism is to argue (as Thomas Hobbes does) that there is nothing but matter in the universe so the mind just is the material brain and there are no mental sensations or ideas, or to argue (as George Berkeley does) that there is nothing but minds and mental sensations and ideas in the universe, so the brain is a construction from mental sensations and ideas.

It is not my purpose here to show in detail how sense-datum philosophy developed. I simply want to point out, and to stress, the fact that Western philosophy at least since Descartes rests on a foundation of immediately perceived sense-data. This is rock bottom both in perception and in certainty. For one cannot deny the immediate and full presence of one's immediate experience of sense-data. As to what causes an immediate sensation (for example, it is commonly presumed that a material body does or can cause a sensation of hardness), or what such a sensation implies (say, the presence of a wall), the causes—material bodies themselves—are inferred, not immediately sensed. In fact, an immediate sensation as such implies nothing beyond itself. It certainly does not imply the existence of a material world or a material cause. So to the extent that one depends on the immediate experience of sense-data for certainty, all knowledge claims other than those pertaining to and resting on immediate sensory experience are uncertain.

But this result constitutes such commonplace knowledge, so obvious as to go generally without mention as one proceeds in the common-sense world of material things, in law court investigations, in the ordinary affairs of life—that it is generally not even noticed. It also is ignored without comment in many (but not all) philosophical and scientific investigations.

A solipsist says it. A solipsist is a throwback to the beginnings of philosophy. A solipsist is a bore, who keeps pointing out that all you know for certain is the immediate sensory data of your consciousness in the present moment. The common-sense philosopher—the solipsist points out—is parading around without any clothes.

To this, most philosophers and scientists say: So what? So what if one can know with absolute certainty only the content of one's consciousness in the present moment? That knowledge is of some, generally trivial, interest. What one is interested in is the uncertain but crucial knowledge of the world about one, the world of bodies and other minds. We (note the plural) want to know how to manipulate things in the world. So one's information about this world is uncertain? So one is even uncertain as to whether it really exists? Again, so what? That's just the way it is. It is adequate for our purposes. *The Cartesian quest for certainty is a will-o-the-wisp.*

Is it? The innocuousness of the anti-certainty "probable is good enough" motif would appear less like whistling in the dark if one had no certain knowledge of anything at all. But in fact, all one's knowledge of immediate sensory data is certain. Any implications drawn about a world of things outside sensory data are uncertain. But that does not detract from the fact that one *does* have certain knowledge about something. One has certain knowledge about one's immediate thoughts and sensory experience in the preset moment. And that knowledge is of immense, crucial, and primary importance to one's life. It constitutes one's being.

Scientific knowledge about material things is uncertain. This is a solid inference from all I have reported above. This conclusion is virtually universally accepted. One can and does live with it. But it does leave open the question of whether or not this uncertain world of bodies actually exists. There is no question that one's immediate sensory impressions and thoughts exist. The solipsist has a certainty about his metaphysical conclusion that his conscious self and what he is conscious of exists, a certainty that the person of common-sense and the scientist do not have about the existence of the world of material bodies and other minds that are postulated in their belief systems.

Yes, yes, yes, the entire philosophical establishment says. We know that. It is boring, boring, boring. We've done away with that fallacy, that trick, that nonsense.

Fallacy? Trick? Nonsense?

What is the fallacy in pointing out that the only existence that one can be certain of is oneself and one's immediate experience? What is the trick in asking what one can be certain of? What is the nonsense in just stating the obvious about one's own experience?

That the search for certainty is nonsense has become dogma in contemporary philosophy. But it is not nonsense. One does have certain knowledge of one's immediate thoughts and sensory experience whenever one is conscious of them. Granted that this certainty is momentary and apparently fleeting, but it is *always* there whenever one thinks about it. If one should make a metaphysics of it, the result is solipsism of the present moment. In fact, of course, the present moment is always now. The persistence through time of the solipsist is an illusion. All that a solipsist can be certain of is that he exists now and has the sensations and ideas he is aware of now.

Who would deny that fact? Oh, philosophers can play around with language games, definitions, ordinary language meanings of words, logical constructions, trick claims about logical consistency, and so on. Wittgenstein originated two language games with which he and many others, both ideal language and ordinary language philosophers, attempt to show that such discussions as this one are nonsense, or are based on mistakes in language use, or simply go nowhere. I don't pursue Wittgenstein's two games because—as he intended—they are designed to go nowhere.

As I remark above, the attempts to construct a logical structure of the world out of sense-data exemplified by Carnap and Goodman are generally considered to be failures. Nevertheless, the constructivist thesis remains embedded in contemporary analytic philosophy. And the empirical thesis that that the foundation of all human knowledge is immediate sensory experience remains.

I show below that the constructivist thesis and its results support the conclusion that the only metaphysical view that can be derived from the only certain knowledge one has is solipsism of the present moment.

Sure, sure, so much the worse for certain knowledge.

I am pointing out another response: So much the worse for Western philosophy.

Am I suggesting that one turn instead to Eastern philosophy? No, even though some Eastern philosophies such as Buddhism have been proposed as being solipsistic. I have looked into the matter just enough to see that Eastern solipsistic philosophies do not begin to be as radical and complete as the solipsism of the present moment that I am describing, or (see below) as the solipsism Santayana describes.

Sense-Datum Philosophy

If solipsism is so overwhelming, why is it so generally ignored or, at best, fobbed off with jokes or scorn? Because it is so overwhelming.

Since Descartes, no Western philosopher has been ignorant of solipsism:

I think, therefore I am. When I am thinking, I exist.

When do I think? In the present moment. When can I know I am thinking? In the present moment. What do I perceive? Sensory images and intelligible ideas. When do I perceive them? Now. When do my memories exist? Now, in the present moment when I am thinking. When can I be certain that I exist? Now, when I am thinking. Could I have come into existence just now, in the immediate present moment? Of course. In fact, the Judeo-Christian foundations of Western philosophy at least since Saint Augustine underlie and provide the ground—even if not always acknowledged—for accepting the possibility that the world as one knows it could have come into existence a moment ago, or just now, and could go out of existence just as momentarily. The Christian God, after all, is said to have created the world out of nothing, and could just as easily reduce it to nothing.

As for the world as one knows it, recognition of the primacy of sense-data goes back to the beginning of Western Philosophy. Plato disdained continuously changing sensory images of odor, taste, sound, touch, and vision, as well as all other passions and thoughts and ideas of which one is immediately conscious. This teaming consciousness is ephemeral and transient in contrast to unchanging Ideas that Plato took to be the eternal forms on which the changing things in our world are based. Later philosophers abandoned the notion of eternal forms. I show above how David Hume analyzed all knowledge into the sensations and ideas perceived in the present moment. The logical analysis of this world whose ontological foundations consist of minimal, momentary sense-data attained dominance with the

Logical Positivism introduced by Moritz Schlick. My thesis is that dependence on sense-data as the elemental building blocks of Modern Philosophy deriving from the Cartesian focus on the immediate data of the senses—has never been, and never can be, overcome.

From roughly the 1930s into the 1980s, philosophy in North America, England, Australia, and parts of northern Europe was dominated by sense-datum Philosophy. It was not called that, but rather was designated as Logical Positivism and later as Analytic Philosophy. This later Analytic Philosophy, after a brief skirmish with so-called Ordinary Language Philosophy, dominates in these precincts today. Its foundations are based on the primary ontological unit of solipsism, the sense-datum.

Rudolf Carnap (1891–1970)

Rudolf Carnap's *The Logical Structure of the World*, first published in 1928, is one of the great books of the twentieth century. It was a bible for several generations of philosophy students, and continues to bear reading as a model of what serious constructive work in analytic philosophy can be. Rereading it now more than fifty years after having been guided through it by Gustav Bergmann, I am again humbled by the intellectual level of Carnap's accomplishment.

Carnap starts with physical objects as ground level. He avoids the use of "material objects" because of the Cartesian implications of "matter." Then he says:

> After we have constructed the physical objects by proceeding from such a physical basis, we can construct the other object types according to our earlier considerations concerning the reducibility of psychological objects to physical ones and of cultural objects to psychological ones. (p. 100)

This sounds as though the ground level of his construction consists of physical objects. These are his primary concern because his construction is designed to provide a logical framework for the physical objects of science. But contrary to the above remark about the "reducibility of psychological objects to physical ones," Carnap in fact reduces both physical objects and cultural objects to psychological objects. These psychological objects are sense-data and intelligible ideas. He continues:

> In selecting a psychological basis, either of the following alternatives is possible: the autopsychological (or "solipsistic") or the general psychological basis. With the autopsychological basis, the available basic elements are restricted to those psychological objects which belong to only *one*

[my italics] subject. As we [I] have seen [say] above, in this case the psychological domain must be divided into two constructionally different parts: from the autopsychological objects [sense data private to one perceiver] we [one] first construct[s] the physical ones, and only then can we [one] construct the heteropsychological objects [sense data common to all perceivers]. If we [one] choose[s] the general psychological basis, then the psychological objects of all psychological subjects are taken as basic elements. (p. 100)

Question: Is it devious, or just cute, that Carnap tries to diminish the sense of the word "solipsistic" by putting it in quotes as though it is odd or not clear, and substituting for it "the general autopsychological basis," as though that virtually opaque expression clarifies what "solipsism" means? Does he just want to avoid pointing out that his position is solipsistic by avoiding the word "solipsism" throughout?

Carnap proclaims without argument that there is a field of heteropsychological public objects consisting of a conglomeration of the private autopsychological objects of a multitude of individual perceivers. The autopsychological objects of each individual perceiver are private sense-data and intelligible ideas. So the logical leap Carnap makes here (the logical flaw that all students of Bergmann were taught to search for) is his assumption that there are such things as public heteropsychological objects made up of the private autopsychological objects of private individual perceivers, for the existence of which public and private objects, and private perceivers, Carnap does not argue. In this procedure, Carnap is also claiming that there is a way to combine all the individual groups of private objects (autopsychologocial sense-data)—each group of which being in fact perceivable only privately by one perceiver and by no other perceivers than that one—into one great group of public objects (heteropsychological sense-data), all of which are perceivable by all perceivers. The logical coherence and thus the actual existence of this combined group of bundles of private individual perceptions into one bundle of publically accessible perceptions is logically impossible. This makes its hypothetical presence as an element in Carnap's construction a major flaw. It destroys the viability of his construction.

Carnap, however, in an attempt to bypass this flaw in his

construction, presents a short disingenuous discourse to the effect that it is a matter of choice whether to begin with the autopsychological or the heteropsychological position.

Well: Why not? It's his system.

In fact, Carnap is perfectly aware that there are no grounds for the public heteropsychological position. So he proceeds:

> In spite of the indicated advantages of the general psychological basis [heteropsychological position], we choose the [individual] autopsychological basis for our constructional system. The most important reason for this lies in our intention to have the constructional system reflect not only the logical-constructional order of the objects, but also their epistemic order. (p. 101)

The epistemic order is the order in which one perceiver knows things. One knows one's private sense-data first, and from it and the assumed private sense-data of many other assumed perceivers, one constructs material bodies. Carnap refers back to this statement:

> An object (or an object type) is called *epistemically primary* [one knows it first in the order of perception] relative to another one, which we call *epistemically secondary*, if the second one is recognized through the mediation of the first and thus presupposes, for its recognition, the recognition of the first. (pp. 88–89)

Again, Carnap starts with [his own] private (autopsychological, solipsistic) sense-data because he cannot perceive public (heteropsychological) sense-data, which he assumes as hypothetical entities constructed from the directly perceived private sense-data of many individual perceivers, whose existence he also must assume. Carnap continues with an apology:

> It is for the same reason that we excluded the system form with physical basis, various versions of which were logically possible. Occasionally, one encounters the opinion that, not autopsychological, but general [hetero]psychological, objects form the basis even in the epistemic order of objects, but this position cannot be maintained in view of

the fact that it is impossible to recognize heteropsychological objects without the mediating recognition of physical
ones.

> The second reason for preferring a system form with an
> autopsychological basis is a formal-logical one. For, even if
> a constructional system with a general psychological basis
> reflected the epistemic order of objects [which in fact it
> does not], a system with an autopsychological basis still
> has the advantage that the totality of all objects is con-
> structed from a considerably smaller basis. (p. 101)

In fact, the autopsychological basis is necessary because only it provides a complete basis for constructing the system. But then to reach
publically perceivable objects, Carnap must contend with the fact
that

> [t]he autopsychological basis is also called *solipsistic*
> [Carnap's italics]. We do not thereby subscribe to the
> solipsistic view that only one subject and its experiences
> are real, while the other subjects are non-real. The differ-
> entiation between real and non-real objects does not stand
> at the beginning of the constructional system. (p. 101)

Carnap's move here is just blatantly to deny the obvious, logical
inference that by starting his constructional system with sense-data
that are private to one individual (the autopsychological basis), the
result is solipsism. He knows that this denial is not justified, so he
goes on to try to avoid solipsism the "bracketing" or phenomenological "withholding of judgment" gambit, as though just setting the
problem aside absolves him of having either to accept or disprove the
obvious solipsistic implication of his autopsychological basis:

> At the beginning of the system, the experiences must sim-
> ply be taken as they occur. We shall not claim reality or
> nonreality in connection with these experiences; rather,
> these claims will be "bracketed" (i.e., we will exercise the
> phenomenological "withholding of judgment") . . . in
> Husserl's sense. (p. 101)

Since the choice of an autopsychological basis amounts merely to an application of the form and method of solipsism, but not to an acknowledgment of its central thesis, we may describe our position as *methodological solipsism.* This viewpoint has been mentioned and expounded in detail, especially by Driesch, as the necessary starting point of epistemology. (p. 102)

But Carnap's use of the phrase "methodological solipsism" to try to avoid the ontological implication that use of the autopsychological basis implies is a pathetic gambit, a trick that does not work. The use of the autopsychological basis cannot be used as a foundation without implying solipsism. If one does withhold, or rather, ignore, the ontological implication of solipsism to construct a system, this means that the construction is not true to the reality of experience as Carnap knows it.

Carnap proceeds on the assumption that he *can* or is permitted to decide which elements in his construction are primary, which is true as long as his construction is no more than a logical exercise. But if his construction is meant to represent the ontological order of experienced being, he is not permitted to decide the order of elements. Then he must begin with private sense-data. And if one does that, the result is solipsism.

This is crucial. To have heteropsychological objects that are publically perceivable by all perceivers, Carnap must have physical objects, which physical objects in turn he says can be derived only from autopsychological objects (private sense-data), each of which is perceivable only to one perceiver. But there is no way to construct publicly perceivable physical objects from privately perceivable solipsistic autopsychological objects. That is, the physical objects Carnap does construct out of private sense-data are not publicly perceivable. They are, bluntly, *Carnap*'s private constructions out of Carnap's private sense-data.

Carnap takes two logical leaps: the first from the private autopsychological sense-data to physical objects (which because of their private source are necessarily private); the second from so-constructed physical objects to purportedly public heteropsychological objects. Carnap describes this process in exactly reverse order:

Statements about physical objects can be transformed into statements about perceptions (i.e., about psychological objects). For example, the statement that a certain body is red is transformed into a very complicated statement which says roughly that, under certain circumstances, a certain sensation of the visual sense ("red") occurs.

Statements about physical objects which are not immediately about sensory qualities can be reduced to statements that are [so reduced]. . . . [A]ll *physical objects are reducible to psychological ones* [Carnap's italics]. (p.92)

The fact this statement actually reports, however, is just the opposite: all physical objects are derived from psychological objects, not "reducible to psychological ones" as Carnap claims. Thus as I tortuously explain above, all so-called physical objects remain private psychological objects.

Finally, Carnap is reduced to the ploy of everyone who cannot refute solipsism: he just denies the facts:

Egocentricity is not an original property of the basic elements [Carnap's italics] of the given. To say that an experience is egocentric does not make sense until we speak of the experiences of others which are constructed from "my" experiences. (pp. 104–5)

This is a standard move of anyone who tries to reject solipsism. Carnap just denies the fact that egocentricity is an original property of the basic elements, which are sense-data. And by saying that an egocentric experience "does not make sense until we speak of the experiences of others" is to blatantly slip in without any justification the assumption that the phrase "experience of others" refers to something that is publically available and needs no justification, when he has not shown that it even makes sense. Carnap simply assumes that conscious beings other than himself exist, and he implies without argument that his private sensations and ideas provide knowledge of other conscious beings. They do not. How could they? Private and public do not overlap, nor can public objects be constructed out of private objects.

In Carnap's case, he follows the standard procedure of analytic philosophers by proceeding with what "must" be the case given the basis of his common-sense ontological assumptions about the existence of many persons or perceivers. But solipsism is based not on what "must" be the case for some logical construction or ontological assumption, but on what one experiences. Although Carnap announces that in his logical construction, "*Egocentricity is not an original property of the basic elements, of the given*" [Carnap's italics] (p. 104), the actual primary impression of the given—as one can determine simply by examining the sensory impressions one experiences—just is its egocentric, autopsychological being. From claiming that it is not, Carnap proceeds that

> To say that an experience is egocentric does not make sense until we speak of the experiences of others which are constructed from "my" experiences. . . . [One must] advance from a subjectless starting point to the construction of experiences which contain the self. . . . A system form with an autopsychological basis is acceptable only because it is recognized that *science is essentially concerned with structure, and that, therefore, there is a way to construct the objective by starting from the individual stream of experience* [Carnap's italics]. Much of the resistance to an autopsychological basis (or "methodological solipsism") can probably be traced back to an ignorance of this fact. (pp. 105–7)

On the contrary, the resistance to an autopsychological basis or to "methodological solipsism" is from the realization that ontologically one must proceed from and on the basis of private sense experience. Thus there is no escape from solipsism, period.

Another trick Carnap uses is to put "my" in quotation marks, to imply or claim that there is no such thing as private sense-data, and then simply to proceed without argument as though it is the case (and perfectly clear) that there is a "subjectless starting point" for "the construction of experiences which contain the self." The moves here are breath-takingly bold. Carnap simply bulldozes over the empirical evidence that one's experience and consciousness begins with a subject, one's self, that has experiences. He reverses the data by saying the empirical starting point is "subjectless" and that one must construct "experiences which contain the self." But on the contrary, the self is primary. The experiences are not constructed but rather are autonomously perceived by the primary self. And if the self is distinct from the experiences, then the self hosts the experiences rather than the experiences containing the self.

Carnap himself continues that

> After deciding to choose an autopsychological basis for our system, (i.e., the acts of consciousness or experiences of the self), we still must determine which entities from this general domain are to serve as basic elements [for constructing physical things and cultural objects]. . . . [W]e do not take the given as it is, but abstractions from it (i.e., something that is epistemologically secondary) as basic elements [for his constructional system]. . . . [I]n perception, the total impression is primary, while sensations and particular feelings, etc., are only the result of an abstracting analysis. (pp. 107–8)

Yes, this is a good description of how Carnap constructs the logical structure of the world, and how he constructs "sensations and particular feelings, etc. [as] only the result of an abstracting analysis." But the steps in his construction do not mirror or describe the actual egocentric experience of the self-consciousness that has, and thus knows, those experiences. The "sensations and particular feelings" are not the result of an "abstracting analysis" at all. They are simply experienced when one is conscious. This is the final point toward which I have been driving: In experience, the solipsistic "sensations and particular feelings" are primary.

The self-conscious person's experiences certainly do provide the material for Carnap's logical construction. But they do not form the foundational elements for a *public* structure of material bodies as Carnap claims. For all its brilliance, Carnap's construction is just that—a construction—and nothing more. It is not a report of what actually takes place in the world. Nor did Carnap mean it to be. But it *is* the world of the autopsychological consciousness, the world of the self-conscious solipsist in the present moment. It is the ontological, metaphysical being of immediate experience that no amount of logical brilliance can alter or erase.

I think that Carnap knew that he was trapped by what he saw as his necessary choice of an autopsychological stance. But he also understood that the only place human knowledge begins is in immediate consciousness. And in immediate consciousness one finds *only* private sensations and intelligible ideas, with no way to derive from them public entities such as physical objects and heteropsychological [public] sensible objects.

Carnap constructed a brilliant logical system for the derivation of public sensible objects, but one cannot find in experience any ground for claiming the existence of such public sensible objects. Once a solipsist, always a solipsist. And Carnap chose as his beginning the autopsychological solipsistic position.

Carnap took the fatal step. Did he not know that the autopsychological stance logically committed him to solipsism? He knew that one cannot simply deny logical conclusions. One cannot simply declare for structural convenience that the solipsistic stance is merely "methodological." The desire to avoid metaphysical commitments is (I contend) one reason why Carnap and the other logical positivists declared all metaphysics to be nonsense. And although solipsism is not nonsense— it makes perfect sense—it is not a position a philosopher of science such as Carnap wants to hold. But there is a conflict here. If all metaphysics is nonsense, and yet the solipsistic stance is necessary to give an exposition of the logical structure of the world, then the whole structure rests on a metaphysical base, the most primary of them all:

> We chose the autopsychological [solipsistic] basis for our constructional system. The most important reason for this lies in our intention to have the constructional system reflect not only the logical-constructional order of the objects, but also their epistemic order. (p. 101)

But the autopsychological or solipsistic basis reflects not just the epistemic, but also the ontological order.

In first edition of *The Logical Structure of the World* of 1928, full-fledged solipsism does not emerge until page 100. Thirty-three years after the appearance of the first edition, in the "Preface to the Second Edition" of 1961, Carnap says:

> The main problem [of this book] concerns the possibility of the rational reconstruction of the concepts of all fields of knowledge on the basis of concepts that refer to the immediately given. . . . [I]t is in principle possible to reduce all concepts to the immediately given. . . . I wanted to attempt . . . the actual formulation of a conceptual system . . . to begin with some simple concepts, for instance sensory qualities and relations, which are present [as] the raw material of experience. . . . The system which is formulated in this book takes as basic elements the elementary experiences. . . . I should now consider for use as basic elements, not elementary experiences . . . but something similar to Mach's elements, e.g., concrete sense-data, as for example "a red of a certain type at a certain visual field place at a given time" [this formulation represents Mach's attempt to depersonalize sense-data]. . . . A system such as the one . . . given in this book has its basis in the "autopsychological domaine" [i.e., private consciousness]. (pp. v–vii)

Then Carnap proceeds immediately with a statement in which he admits that his whole constructive project fails:

> The positivist thesis of the reducibility of thing concepts to autopsychological [private sense-datum] concepts remains valid, but the [opposite] assertion that the [physical thing concepts] can be defined in terms of the [autopsychological concepts] must now be given up. . . .

But he continues in apparent denial of his first sentence in this quotation:

> and hence also that all statements about things can be translated into statements about sense-data. (p. viii)

Carnap does not alter his second-edition text to substantiate this last claim. He could not do this without destroying his construction. My

90

interpretation is that in the years between 1928 and 1961, it became painfully obvious to Carnap that by adopting the autopsychological standpoint, he committed himself to ontological, metaphysical solipsism. There is no way out, so he reverted to use of the constructivist rock-bottom method: bold pronouncement. After all, if all metaphysics is nonsense, then so are any inferences that result in metaphysical commitments.

This solipsistic interpretation of Carnap is presented as commonplace and obvious by Herbert Feigl in his essay "The 'Mental' and the 'Physical'" (1958) in which he says that

> phenomenological descriptions of momentary direct experience . . . represent the extreme lower limit of cognition; they constitute, admittedly, a "degenerate" and "highly impoverished" sort of knowledge. Nevertheless, they are the "ultimate" basis of all our empirical knowledge claims. It is in this sense , and in this sense only, that I countenance a "methodological solipsistic" (or "ego-centric") reconstruction. The data of direct experience provide the ultimate confirming or disconfirming evidence of all our factual knowledge. (p. 149)

Nelson Goodman (1906–1998)

In 1966 in *The Structure of Appearance*, Nelson Goodman sets out, as did Rudolf Carnap before him, to construct a logical representation of the world as it appears to one in immediate sensory experience. The foundational, primary, elementary entities or elements in this construction (again as for Carnap) are private sense-data, construed as the smallest perceptible sensations of touch, taste, sound, odor, and sight, which five-some, as always, is representative of the immense number of nuanced sensations, ideas, passions, etc., in one's consciousness.

> Choice of a phenomena list basis is usually argued from the ground that since the phenomenal by its very nature comprises the entire content of immediate experience, everything that can be known at all must be eventually explicable in terms of phenomena.

> In the first place, a phenomenalist system . . . takes some perceptible phenomenal individuals as its basic units. . . . In the second place, speaking from outside a phenomenalist system, one may describe its basis as solipsistic, may say that its basic units are comprised within a single stream of experience. (p. 37)

This is the high road to solipsism. But like Carnap, Goodman proceeds immediately as though he can ignore the implications of beginning with this solipsistic standpoint, and simply pronounce that

> But speaking from the point of view of the system itself, this is an anachronism. For the basic units of such a system are not taken as belonging to a subject and representing an object. They are taken as elements in terms of which must be constructed whatever objects, subjects, streams of

experience, or other entities the system talks about at all. (pp. 141–42)

I want to make clear that I do understand what Goodman is doing. Goodman (and Carnap) admit, even announce, that sense-data are private to a perceiver, that no sense-data are in fact shared with other perceivers, and that a sense-datum system logically implies solipsism. But they dismiss this implication as being irrelevant or as having no logical force or as unintelligibly metaphysical or as just plain ridiculous, and proceed boldly with definitions of public sense-data that can be perceived by more than one perceiver. They do this despite the fact that the very notion of public sense-data is blatantly contradictory. Sense-data are by their very nature private.

Goodman continues immediately by *proclaiming* that

> These basic [sense-datum] units are *neutral* [his italics] material. A [sensory] presentation, for example, may be at once part of a stream of phenomena and part of a physical object; but this will depend on later constructions of the system. Aside from all such questions however, it is clear that whatever are the differences among whatever persons there are, the constructions of a phenomenalistic system are discussed and tested quite as intersubjectively as those of any other system. (p. 142)

Here he again blatantly *decrees* that that a phenomenalistic system, which is constructed from private sense-data, can be discussed and tested intersubjectively. Sure, I have been discussing such systems—those of Carnap and Goodman—myself. But test them *intersubjectively*? No.

Goodman sets as his primary entities private objects of experience—sense-data—that are ontologically restricted to one perceiver. But then he hypothesizes intersubjective elements that can be experienced by any number of perceivers. But the only way he can introduce intersubjective elements into his system is by grouping together the private subjective elements of several perceivers, and such combining does not result in intersubjective elements.

Goodman calls on Carnap for support:

Carnap has given notice that his system would be phenomenalistic and thus in *one sense* solipsistic: [Goodman is
squirming here, trying to mitigate the impact of "solipsistic" with the weasel phrase *one sense*: actually, for Carnap
there is only one sense] but he has pointed out that strictly the ground elements (i.e., the basic units) are subjectless,
since such terms as "subject," "subjective," and "objective" have to be defined at a later stage in the system.
Although the system is solipsistic in a loose sense [all this
means is that solipsism is not taken seriously], it by no
means embodies a '*solipsism of the present moment*' [my
italics]. It commences with a set of [full momentary cross
sections of the total stream of the experiences of all existing perceivers] that together exhaust the total temporally
long stream of experience. That does not solve the problem of ordering the [cross-sections] in time, nor of distinguishing past, present, and future; but it does make unnec-
essary, for instance, the construction of past experience
solely in terms of memory images and other present experience [as Hume does]. (p. 154)

But then Goodman goes on in fact to appeal to minimal sense qualia:

If we divide the stream of experience into its smallest concrete parts and then go on to divide these concreta into
sense qualia, we arrive at entities suitable as atoms for a
realistic system. (p. 189)

These "sense qualia" are what are ordinarily referred to as sense-
data. They are private to each perceiver. The "stream of experience"
Goodman refers to is what he hypothesizes as the total collection of
private sense-data had by all private perceivers. He thus reverses the
process of starting with private sense-data and combining them into
a collection of the private sense-data had by many perceivers.

But where did the collection of private sense-data come from?
Apparently from all the private perceivers. Goodman is assuming
that there is more than one (himself) private perceiver. And he is
assuming that somehow, the private perceptions of many private

perceivers can be collected together, and that someone (he himself to construct his system) can perceive the entire collection. But of course he cannot perceive other people's private perceptions.

Now quickly to quench the immediate objection of analytic philosophers: I know that Goodman would claim to have a perfect right to make this move. He is, for goodness sakes, simply *talking* about these private sense-data. He isn't claiming to perceive other people's private sense-data.

Right. But to construct his public world-system, he *is* presuming that this great collection of many bundles of private sense-data exists. Out of them he will construct public physical objects. This is all very nice, but the crucial element ignored by Goodman here is the fact that there is no evidence whatsoever that there is more than one existing bundle of private sense-datum perceptions. One's own at the present moment. One cannot construct a world of public physical objects from private sense-data, not from a huge collection of them from many people, and most certainly not from the small collection of private sense-data from the only collection one knows for certain to exist: one's own.

But, my critic says, with greatly restrained annoyance, let the man go about his construction.

OK.

Like Carnap, Goodman proceeds by assuming that solipsism is not true. He admits that he must start with solipsism, and even that he cannot refute the evidence for it, but then he just puts it aside—as has done virtually every Western philosopher since Descartes who has faced the problem.

I have above described solipsism of the present moment in which presently perceived memory qualia account for one's impression of time having passed. It is quite simple to focus on present experience as being composed of a myriad of minimal qualia in all modes of perception (sound, smell, taste, feeling, and vision), although one seldom does so. But, still, all this perceived sense-data is private and in the present moment. It leaves the logical constructions of Carnap and Goodman hanging free. It isn't solipsism that results in Cloud-Cuckoo land, it is the Carnap-Goodman construction of the public physical world out of the combined private sense-data of many perceivers.

Well, I'll get on with it. All I am concerned with here is the experiential fact that one's sensory fields at the present moment can easily be viewed as consisting of myriad minimal qualia. (I remark below about Herbert Spiegelberg's phenomenological workshop in which this was done.) Goodman concurs. He takes for the atoms of his construction, "qualia":

> Our atoms . . . "qualia"—are to be such qualities as single phenomenal colors, sounds, degrees of warmth, moments, and visual locations . . . a realistic system treats all individuals as made up of qualities . . . even the most concrete individuals are to be defined in terms of qualia. (pp. 199–200)

However, Goodman goes on to say:

> I do not suppose that qualia are the 'original' givens and . . . doubt whether the question of what is originally given in experience can even be made clear. (p. 263)

Goodman is being disingenuous here. Focusing on the sensory elements or qualia in one's sensory fields is quite simple to do, as is considering minimal qualia in each sensory field. Of course the results are not mathematically precise, but I have had hundreds of students over the years who get the point. To say that they really do not understand, or do not perceive what they claim to perceive is highly condescending.

For many years one of my colleagues was the phenomenalogist Herbert Spiegleberg. For several summers he conducted phenomenological workshops for visiting professors and graduate students in which they worked to isolate and describe sensory phenomena as they really perceived it. I sat in on some sessions. It is not difficult at all to focus on minimal perceptions in the present moment. Yes, I know some people deny this possibility outright. Goodman allows it:

> The advocate of "solipsism of the present moment" confines himself to the experience of one moment. Others may complain that he chooses each different moment as it occurs, and that every time he says that all experience is present, he proclaims a different thesis since each

96

"present" refers to a different moment. But for him there is only a single moment; his position depends upon denying that there are any phenomenal temporal distinctions. Now the apparent futility of trying to construct any adequate system based on the experience of a single moment is not itself a conclusive argument against him. One has no alternative but to strive for such a system if convinced that there is only a single time quale. (pp. 376–77)

This is a fair description of solipsism of the present moment. And Goodman ignores that Hume does account for the sense of time having passed, which sense is perceived in the present moment. Goodman, however, goes on:

But it seems to me quite as evident that phenomenal temporal distinctions *are* made—that several time qualia are discerned [does he mean that a series of sequentially successive time qualia are discerned at the same time, or that several moments are discerned at the same time?]—as that several place qualia and several color qualia are discerned. Thus I think we are not confined to the experience of a single moment [apparently that is what he means]. (p. 377)

First, of course, it is incoherent to speak of perceiving several moments at the same moment, so Goodman speaks of conscious perception extending over several moments. Perhaps. This would extend solipsism of the present moment to solipsism of a few moments. It makes more sense and is cleaner—logically and systemically speaking—to explain the sense of passing time as Hume does, with memory qualia.

What purpose do these logical constructions serve? It seemed important to Carnap and Goodman to construct logical systems beginning with primary elements of perception (sense-data), which systems represent the logical structure of the sensory world that is our only direct contact with what they take to be the real world (or worlds) of common-sense and science: tables and chairs, atoms and sub-atomic particles. They are clear, if not very forthcoming, about the fact that one never has any direct experience of tables, chairs, atoms, and sub-atomic particles. Carnap does not think it worth commenting on. Goodman devotes the last pages of his book (pp. 378–80) to "The Physical World," in which he says:

> [A]ccounting for the physical world upon a phenomenalistic basis [the foundational basis of his construction] . . . is out of bounds for us here . . . [and] it is widely regarded as insoluble and its insolubility is often taken as sufficient reason for completely abandoning the phenomenalistic approach. (p. 378)

Obviously Goodman cannot admit outright that the problem of "accounting for the physical world upon a phenomenalistic basis" is insoluble, because his entire construction is posed as the foundation for such an accounting:

> In my view, the systematic description of phenomena as such provides genuine answers to important problems; and also the methods developed for accomplishing such a description may often serve as models for the treatment of parallel problems within the objective realm. (p. 370)

These important problems do not include the problem of

> accounting for the physical world upon a phenomenalistic basis. [Instead,] the methods developed for accomplishing such a description *may* [my italics] often serve as models for the treatment of parallel problems within the objective realm. (p. 379)

Goodman is rightfully not one who is congenitally modest about his own logical abilities and accomplishments. So it is sobering to see him not meeting the problem of "accounting for the physical world upon a phenomenalistic basis" by saying that the distinction between phenomenalistic and physicalistic predicates is not altogether sharp (p. 379), and proceeding:

> In the second place, is the physical world that we are to explain the somewhat inconsistent world of common-sense and stale science or the very abstruse and continually revised world of the latest physical theory? . . . Our explicandum is not so plainly before us that systematic

explanation can proceed without a good deal of prior clar- ification and criticism. In the third place, we saw that tra ditional criteria of definition are hardly applicable even to some of the most elementary and most obviously satisfac- tory definitions of a constructional system. (pp. 379–80)

Why, then, has Goodman constructed his system? The answer lies in the last paragraph of his book.

What does seem to be fairly clear is that the problem is intimately connected with the problem of distinguishing between laws and nonlaws, of interpreting counterfactual conditionals, and of codifying the principles of confirma- tion. In recent investigations of these problems some very discouraging difficulties have arisen. But it is worth noting that these difficulties arise primarily in dealing with a nat- ural language and are greatly diminished within a con- structional system where control can be maintained over the predicates admitted. (p. 380)

Goodman does pursue some of these problems, but remains far from "accounting for the physical world on a phenomenalistic basis."

My point here is in part to show how far in fact the logical con- structions on a phenomenalistic basis by Carnap and Goodman are from actually providing a foundation for representing the physical world. But also, I am stressing the fact that what is immediately empirically available to human consciousness, what is directly per- ceived, what is known for certain to exist, is entirely and only the sen- sations and ideas of one's own consciousness in the present moment.

Gilbert Ryle (1900–1996)

Gilbert Ryle is one of many philosophers who, like Goodman, admit that the contents of one's consciousness are private in the sense that only oneself can have direct acquaintance with those contents—sensations, ideas, thoughts, feelings, and so on—but then blithely with no apology whatsoever proceed by assuming the existence of other minds, objects of naïve realism such as tables and chairs, and of the common-sense universe of many minds and bodies.

Such philosophers obviously believe that the solipsistic implications of the private content of one's consciousness, and the fact that one never encounters other minds or material objects, are silly or at least not to be taken seriously. So Carnap and Goodman simply declare by fiat explicitly or implicitly that publicly accessible sense-data are available and then go about constructing the physical world out of them. In *The Concept of Mind*, Ryle proposes to avoid the implications of privacy by examining

> the logical geography of concepts . . . to show why certain sorts of operations with the concepts of mental powers and processes are breaches of logical rules. . . . The key arguments employed in this book are therefore intended to show why certain sorts of operations with the concepts of mental powers and processes are breaches of logical rules. I try to use *reductio ad absurdum* arguments both to disallow operations implicitly recommended by the Cartesian myth [of mind and matter] and to indicate to what logical types the concepts under investigation ought to be allocated. . . Philosophy is the replacement of category-habits by category-disciplines. . . . . Primarily I am trying to get some disorders of my own system. Only secondarily do I hope to help other theorists to recognize our malady and to benefit from my medicine. (pp. 8–9)

Carnap and Goodman believed that they could solve philosophical problems by designing ideal language logical systems in which these problems are avoided. Ryle is a major member of another group who believed that many (if not all) philosophical problems are the result of misuse of ordinary language. One such misuse according to Ryle is what he calls "Descartes' Myth," the view that every human being consists of a union of mind and body. Ryle also refers to Descartes's position as

> 'the dogma of the Ghost in the Machine' [which is] a category-mistake. It represents the facts of mental life as if they belonged to one logical type or category (or range of types or categories) when they actually belong to another. (pp. 15–16)

Ryle's basic argument is that

> the phrase 'there occur mental processes' does not mean the same sort of thing as 'there occur physical processes', and therefore . . . it makes no sense to conjoin or disjoin the two. (p. 22)

Here I intend to give just a taste (now there is a category mistake) of Ryle's method and of the kind of language analysis he undertakes to claim that Descartes's mind-body problem is dissolved when one gets language use right. Perhaps Ryle is right and there is no mind-body problem. But he does not deny that there is a solipsism problem:

> It is, of course, true and important that I am the only person who can give a first-hand account of the tweaks given me by my ill-fitting shoe, and an oculist who cannot speak my language is without his best source of information about my visual sensations. But the fact that I alone can give first-hand accounts of my sensations does not entail that I have, what others lack, the opportunity of observing these sensations [although] there is a philosophically unexciting though important sense of 'private' in which of course my sensations are private or proprietary to me [but]

it is nonsense to speak of observing, inspecting, witnessing, or scrutinizing sensations, since the objects proper to such verbs are things and episodes. (p. 209)

Right: "there is a philosophical unexciting though important sense of 'private' in which of course my sensations are private or proprietary to me." That is the ground of solipsism. But, Ryle announces that "It is nonsense to speak of observing, inspecting, witnessing, or scrutinizing sensations, since the objects proper to such verbs are things and episodes." Oh? That grammatical correction dispenses with solipsism—right? I am reminded of the famous philosopher, Humpty-Dumpty: "It's a question of who's to be master. You or the words."

The way Ryle tries to escape the solipsistic implications of the privacy of conscious experience is by analyzing language use. One problem with this method is that language philosophers are famous for disagreeing about language use. One technique, in fact, is working through so many different possibilities that the person whose position is being analyzed gives up, and this solves the problem through exhaustion.

Such analyses of language produced with the intent of solving such metaphysical problems as Descartes's mind-body problem are often called "language games." But these analyses have no force at all for use in denying the privacy of sensations and ideas as they are experienced. It becomes a game to talk one's way out of solipsism, although as the quotation above shows, Ryle and "ordinary language" philosophers cannot deny the fact of private experiences, no more than can "ideal language" philosophers such as Carnap and Goodman define their way to notions of public sense experiences.

I make the following disclaimer several times in this book: I do not purport to explain the origins of one's sensory and intellectual experience. If they have a cause, I don't know what it is, nor do I even know if they have a cause. I simply present and consider one's sensory and intellectual experience as it is, as it occurs, in one's consciousness. I do not construct a logical system to incorporate one's private experience into a public system, nor do I analyze either ordinary or scientific language to explain away its private nature as it appears to one. One's private experience is what it is. The private nature of its appearance cannot be "explained away." My point is that I am not "doing philosophy" at all. I am simply describing the private experience one has that leads one to postulate the thesis of solipsism of the present moment.

Just as I had in my graduate school years three wonderful professors—Robert Turnbull (philosophical analysis), Gustav Bergmann (logical positivism) and Richard Popkin (skepticism)—as I remark above, I also had as a colleague for many years the famous phenomenologist, Herbert Spiegelberg. For many summers, Spiegelberg conducted workshops for professors and post-graduate students in descriptive phenomenology. As I remarked above, I sat in on some of the sessions. He would, for example, put a lighted candle on a table in a darkened room, and then all the participants sitting around that table were charged with describing what they saw phenomenologically. Not the candle—the phenomena. There is a lot there to see and experience. And in such a study, one can focus on separate qualia or sense-data.

What I ask you to do is to focus on the experienced content of your consciousness. Is it possible for one to experience the content of anyone else's consciousness? No, of course not. The privacy of one's own experience is primary. Sometimes this privacy is a delight and a consolation. Sometimes such privacy leads to despair. One knows for certain however that in one's consciousness, one is alone in the solipsism of the present moment.

Analytical Solipsism

In this brief résumé of a few classic treatments of solipsism I make no attempt to cover the waterfront, but I do try to examine the best representative works. Here I examine *Analytical Solipsism* by William Todd. This fine book has been virtually ignored. Unfortunately, from the beginning, Todd dismisses solipsism as a serious metaphysical position. Nevertheless, he makes some worthwhile comments. Todd begins:

> At some points in the history of philosophy the solipsist has been one who denied the existence of everything except himself or even the existence of everything except his own present sensations. At other times, the solipsist instead of doubting these things has merely insisted that there could be no good reason for believing in the existence of anything beyond one's own present sensations. Roughly, this doubt is aimed at reason rather than at things. A solipsist of this sort appears in Santayana's *Skepticism and Animal Faith*. . . . The modern solipsist . . . instead of denying the existence of an irreducible physical world . . . tells us that we never believed in it anyway. (p. vii)

Todd works in the sense-datum tradition. He says that physical objects are never perceived directly, but rather indirectly by way of the direct, conscious apprehension of mental sensations. He says that "there are no inherent qualitative differences between images and sensations" (p. 17). He continues that

> the solipsist's main thesis is that everything which can ordinarily be said could, in theory, be said in a language which referred only to one's own sensations. (p. 24)

Unless Todd takes "sensations" to range over the entire mental content of the mind (which he does not), then this restriction does not encompass full-fledged solipsism. He bases his objections to solipsism on the Wittgensteinian assumption that one has to learn language from other people in the existing external world. But the solipsist denies that there is any evidence that there is a world external to his thoughts. The solipsist does not have to account for the fact that he *seems* to have learned language from other people. He does not have to explain the phenomena of his private experience at all, nor does he try to. All the solipsist needs to do is accept the world of phenomena as he experiences it. And I take it as my task here to explain the solipsist's grounds for describing the world as he experiences it.

What Todd and virtually all philosophers who dismiss solipsism do not or claim not to recognize is that the solipsist is *sui generis*, unique, a kind in itself. The solipsist appears to himself complete, with his sensations and ideas, in the present moment. The solipsist does not know, or need to know, the source of his existence. In fact, the solipsist—as Hume points out—does not need a source. The solipsist just is.

Todd, like so many opponents of solipsism, assumes or infers that the solipsist must have a source, an origin, a background. Then Todd, like so many philosophers, wants to *explain* the presence of the solipsist. This is to view the solipsist as being in or having originated in the common-sense world of common-sense objects.

But the solipsist is not an entity in the world of common-sense. The solipsist is not a material thing. The solipsist does not even exist in the temporal world of passing time. The solipsist exists only now, at the present moment. The major problem with the literature on solipsism is that virtually no one recognizes or accepts the ontological status of the solipsist as it really is. The solipsist is a private, timeless entity that exists without a cause only in the present moment.

Like Carnap and Goodman, Todd begins by denying the thesis—the radical nature—of solipsism. This denial is based in part on Todd's assumption that one can have a language only if it is learned through public interaction with people and a world independent of one's own conscious experience. But this is both to misunderstand solipsism, and to assume that solipsism is impossible. It is to assume that there is a (material) world separate from one's own (mental) thoughts, a world that acts on one's mind and that is necessary for one to learn a language (about that world).

But the solipsist just is. The solipsist finds himself in the world, with all he knows, with his experiences and understandings. The solipsist appears to have come into being, because here he is. Perhaps he had a cause, but maybe not. Nothing in his present being or experience requires that he had or had to have a cause.

This is not absurd unless you think God has to exist to have caused the universe. But if you think that, you have the problem of how God came into being. God caused himself? Fine. Maybe the solipsist caused himself. Why not? One who professes solipsism is often accused of thinking or implying that he is God. If the solipsist wise-cracks back that he would have made his existence more pleasant than it is if he had caused himself, he misunderstands himself. He did not cause himself to be. As far as that goes, why should the solipsist need a cause? He just finds himself to be. Moreover, it does not follow that if one created oneself, and thus one's world, the world would be more pleasant than one finds it to be. The world God is said to have created could have been more pleasant than it is, too.

One does not have to postulate a cause for the existence of the solipsist. The solipsist may not have a cause, nor even a beginning, as far as that goes. Some scientists argue that the entire universe had a beginning, but not a cause. Whatever.

The need to go through all that is an indication of how pathetic most supposed refutations and rejections of solipsism are. Here one is, with one's consciousness, thoughts, and language. Their existence is simply a fact. Inferences about what is required for one to have consciousness, thoughts, and language are irrelevant. Ludwig Wittgenstein and numerous others following him (see Héctor-Neri Castañeda) tried that gambit in arguing against private language. Language is, they argue, necessarily public. It was developed, and had to be developed, they claim, in the evolution of communication among human beings. But this is simply to beg the question. If one does exist as a solipsist who *does* have what might be termed a private language (because there are no other existing minds), then all the logic-chopping about what having a language implies or requires in terms of other minds cannot take it away. No analysis of language in itself—which is all one can do in attempting to demonstrate how or prove that it developed, or had to develop, through people with separate minds talking to one another—no analysis of the structure or use of language itself can prove that it was, or had to be, developed through the linguistic interaction of a number of communicating conscious minds. In fact, of course, the solipsist does not have to provide any proofs or reasons or procedures to explain or justify his possession of language. He just has the sensations and ideas and mental powers—including knowledge of language.

Like Carnap and Goodman, Todd goes about devising a logical structure of a system devoted to the explanation of how—from sensing sense-data—one can construct a world of material bodies and other minds.

These constructivists simply assume that material things external to one's mind exist. And they assume that one can have sensations and ideas only through the interaction of one's mind with those external bodies. But this is a baseless assumption of what is to be proved—that there is a world external to one's mind.

The solipsist begins (and ends) with his sensations and ideas, his experience. He does not have to construct a system to explain how he got those sensations and ideas. He emphatically does not have to assume the existence of an external material world. The solipsist is not a sense-datum philosopher. Explicitly, the solipsist does not have to construct (as Carnap and Goodman do) a material world out of sense-data. His world is complete as it is.

It might be said that I am trying to make vehement pronouncement do the work of argument. Not at all. I am not presenting arguments, and do not intend to. I am just stating the facts about the world in which the solipsist finds himself.

I doubt that it is impossible to overstate this point. The burden does not lie on the solipsist to show how one can construct or get to know a public external world on the basis of his acquaintance with private sense-data. The burden rests on the proponent of a public external world to give evidence that there is or need be such an external world. Carnap and Goodman certainly knew this point. If they deviated around the problem of defeating solipsism, they certainly tried to construct a logical system that would charm other philosophers into forgetting about or dismissing solipsism. But if there were ever a non-metaphysical philosopher (as logical positivists claimed to be), it is the solipsist. The solipsist is a realist.

The solipsist begins and ends with the world of his thoughts. Solipsism is a lonely philosophy. On the other hand, this fact does not change the solipsist's basic world experience, which remains the same as it would be if there were a public world populated by many other minds as is postulated (explicitly or implicitly) by all other philosophers.

All other philosophers? How can a solipsist say that? There are not any other philosophers according to the solipsist. Well, possibly not. But nothing restricts the possibility that there could be many solipsists. There is no reason to suppose, for example, that a solipsist takes up space, given that space is just a figment of the solipsist's mind. There is plenty of room for a myriad of solipsists.

As already discussed, time also is just a figment of the solipsist's mind. His sense of continuity of being and experience is expressed in his *present* experience and his *present* memories and imaginations, the memories *as* being about events that happened in the past, the imaginations *as* being about things that might happen in the future. But the solipsist himself always exists in the present moment as do also, again, the aspect of pastness in his memories and the aspect of futureness in his mental projections. The solipsist and his memories, present sensations, and ideas of future experiences all exist only in the present. Now.

How can you doubt it?

I provide a description of solipsism and the solipsist, not an explanation. Scientists search for explanations, but an ontologist need only describe what appears to be the case. An ontologist need not explain brute facts.

The brute fact about solipsism is that it is and it is private. There is no public. Solipsism cannot be refuted either logically or empirically. So it is passed over, ignored, joked about, set aside, closeted. Solipsism is the embarrassment of Western philosophy.

However, the irrefutability of solipsism just is *the fundamental question of human existence*. The notion of a public world is incoherent. The existence of a public world cannot be explained and cannot be confirmed.

Todd admits that one is confined to one's own thoughts, to one's own sensory experiences and ideas. He sees the solipsist's task then to be one of analyzing the statements of ordinary language in terms of statements about one's own sensations and ideas. Like Carnap and Goodman, Todd wants to construct a language adequate to the languages of common-sense and of science. Todd says that

> In our system the primitive terms will be chosen in such a way that . . . they will refer to sensations, and the axioms will then be statements that ultimately talk about sensations . . . the function of philosophy is just to give directions for axiomatizing our beliefs about the world [and] since different persons are in different situations and have differing beliefs about the world, there would have to be somewhat different sets of axioms for each person. Further, since we accumulate more information as time goes on and lose other information, the axiom system might have to be *for* a particular person *at* a particular time. However, if our directions were followed all such axioms would ultimately talk about a person's own sensations. Hence our system will be solipsistic in that the axioms refer to such a limited scope of phenomena. (p. 158)

This is exuberant. To avoid solipsism, Todd conceives of a world of many persons, each of whom is a solipsist in the sense of being confined to direct knowledge and acquaintance only with the thoughts—the sensations and ideas—in that person's own consciousness. Then "the function of philosophy is just to give directions for axiomatizing our beliefs about the world" (p. 158). But this axiomatization has been done by Carnap and Goodman at a level of rigor and finesse much higher than that exhibited by Todd, so I leave him here.

George Santayana (1863–1952)

Only one philosopher has ever defended solipsism at length and in depth. In the first 100 pages of *Skepticism and Animal Faith* published in 1924, George Santayana gives a brilliant, irrefutable exposition and defense of solipsism. He concludes that no one can believe in solipsism, and then he spends 200 more pages at doomed-to-failure attempts to deny (but not to refute) it. His is an heroic attempt. Never mind, the great philosopher-poet concludes. One is constitutionally determined to live as though there exists a common-sense public material world in which minds are linked to animal bodies beyond the private, ephemeral sensations and ideas that one admittedly has. Animal faith is just the irresistibly driven urge to behave as though—and even to believe that—the true world is the world of common-sense, the world of material bodies, like one's own, and of other minds, like one's own. There is, Santayana admits, no actual evidence for the existence either of a material world or of other minds or for that matter of one's own mind. One believes in their existence instinctively, solely on the grounds of animal faith.

Here follows an exposition of Santayana's brilliant analysis and irrefutable defense of solipsism. On the one hand, it is difficult to conceive of a more complete and definitive exposition of and argument for solipsism. On the other hand, Santayana's poetic prose is so far removed from what passes for clarity among today's analytic philosophers that I suspect few of them would have the patience to decipher those 100 pages. I shall do it for them.

In his *Skepticism and Animal Faith* (1923), George Santayana begins:

> Any solipsism which is not a *solipsism of the present moment* [my italics] is logically contemptible. The postulates on which empirical knowledge and ineffective science are based—namely, that there has been a past, that it was

such as it is now thought to be, that there will be a future and that it must, for some inconceivable reason, resemble the past and obey the same laws—these are all gratuitous dogmas. . . .

[One] may perhaps have images before him of scenes somehow not in the foreground, with a sense of before and after running through them; and he may call this background of his sentiency the past [but] those outlying regions and those reported events . . . are pure fancy. . . . The solipsist thus becomes an incredulous spectator of his own romance, thinks his own adventures fictions, and accepts a *solipsism of the present moment.* [my italics] (pp. 14–15)

Santayana argues that this solipsism of the present moment is thrust upon one.

Turn whichever way I will, and refine as I may, the pressure of existence, of absolute tyrannical present being seems to confront me. Something is evidently going on, at least in myself. I feel an instant complex stream of existence, forcing me to say that I think and that I am. (p. 21)

The ordinary reader or Western philosopher might object that no such intensity of present experience is apparent to him, and certainly this is true of most of one's experience. It is possible that one might never recognize that one's experience is confined only to the present moment. But once one does become aware of the immediacy of one's experience, one realizes that it appears only in the present moment:

Another thing is the *belief* [Santayana's italics] that what is found in [immediate experience] is a report or description of events that have happened already, in such manner that the earlier phases of the flux I am aware of existed first, before the later phases and without them; whereas in my intuition now the earlier phases are merely the first part of the given whole, exist only together with the later phases, and are earlier only in a perspective, not in a flux of successive events. . . . The unity of apperception which

111

yields the sense of change renders change specious, by relating the terms and directions of change together in a single perspective, as respectively receding, passing, or arriving. (p. 25)

Thus, one's consciousness is always of the present. What one perceives are always present sensations that give the sense of change. That is, the sense of time passing is in the present. But in fact, these perceptions are present perceptions, in the specious present, like all others.

Santayana continues:

You feel you have changed; you feel things changing? Granted. Does this fact help you feel an earlier state which you do not [now] feel, which is not an integral part of what is now before you, but a state from which you are supposed to have passed into the state in which you now are? If you feel that earlier state now, there is no change involved. That datum, which you designate as the past, and which exists only in this [present] perspective, is merely a term in your present feeling. *It was never anything else* [my italics]. It was never given otherwise than as it is given now, when it is given as past . . . every suggestion of a past is false. (pp. 28–29)

Santayana's solipsism of the present moment is like that of David Hume. Hume supports his temporally stationary solipsism with the denial that there is any causal power in the universe. And this follows from his claim that there are no substances, neither minds nor bodies, in the universe. Nothing changes. Existence is like a whirlwind that appears to be moving forward, but it is in fact stationary, as is all existence, stationary and momentary—there is no flow. One's existence rests on the crest of a breaking wave.

From this perspective, it can be seen that Russell, Carnap, Goodman, and others construct a world out of sense-data to escape the solipsism that is implied by the private nature of sense-data. They ignore or deny the private nature of individual consciousness and its contents. Santayana never denies the existence of this so-called solipsistic predicament, never tries to escape from it. The word "predicament" is used to imply that it can be escaped. It cannot. In such an attempt to escape solipsism, philosophers such as Carnap and Goodman ignore or deny the private nature of individual consciousness and its contents.

After a hundred pages of exposition and discussion of solipsism of the present moment, Santayana abandons it for what he calls animal faith, the instinctive belief that one has an animal body and that there is a natural world of material bodies that change through time:

> That such external things exist, that I exist myself [as a thing persisting but also changing through time] and live more or less prosperously in the midst of them, is a faith not founded on reason but precipitated in action, and in that intent, which is virtual action, involved in perception. . . . [I have reached] the apex of skepticism . . . intending presently to abandon it for common-sense. (pp. 106, 108)

In those first hundred pages, Santayana brilliantly defends the thesis that the solipsist exists only atemporally in the present moment. All sense of flow of time or of events or of sensations and ideas is an illusion manifested in the present moment. This is the direct contrary to the natural world of animal faith. Thus Santayana's embrace (in the last two hundred pages of his book) of the common-sense temporal, changing world of animal faith appears as an embarrassed cop-out in the context of his book as a whole.

In fact, Sanatayana is not abandoning the solipsistic conclusions of his reasoning. Instead, in the last two-thirds of his book, I see Santayana indulging the sensibility that later led him to write five volumes of *The Realms of Being*, poetic, even romantic, constructions of an imaginary world, that is, of the world as he imagined he lived in it. Thus he says that

> the existence of intuition is tantamount to that of a self . . . the pure spirit involved in any intuition of essence . . . is repeatedly and . . . consecutively actualized in a running mental discourse. (p. 147)

As this quotation shows, as one proceeds through the last two thirds of *Animal Faith*, one recognizes the bones of solipsism of the present moment sticking through. Santayana always qualifies his common-sense constructions of realms of being.

> Mind and memory are . . . names for almost the same thing. . . . [T]his sensation . . . of having lived up to the present, is a primary memory. It sets up a temporal perspective, believing firmly in its recessional character: parts of the specious present are interpreted as survivals of a receding present. . . . Memory deploys all the items of its inventory at some [temporal] distance, yet sees them directly, by a present glance. . . . [T]he sentiment of pastness [is] the receding perspective in which memory places its data. (pp. 150–51)

> Memory is a reconstruction, not a relapse (p. 156)

As for the plausibility of the common-sense world of animal faith, Santayana says:

> How can [temporal] flux be observed at all? If flux there be, the earlier part is gone when the latter part appears. . . . [I]f its being is instantaneous, there is no flux. . . . [A] sense of change, falling necessarily under a unity of apperception, transcends that change . . . mind, by its very character, is timeless. . . . [S]pirit is not in time . . . the perception of flux [or of anything else] is not a flux, but a synthetic glance and a single intuition of relation of form, of quality. (p. 161)

> All intuition . . . in one sense may be said always to be . . . instantaneous. (p. 196)

This last comment is the most difficult stumbling block for comprehension of solipsism of the present moment. There is no passing time. There are only the sensations, images, and experience of the present moment. Because there is no passing of time, no succession of self-conscious moments, every moment is the only moment there is, was, or will be. In that sense, the present self-conscious moment is also the last moment there will ever be. One lives ones life in this stationary state. It just does not seem to one that the present moment is the only moment there is. The reason for this is the existence of memories in the present moment, memories that give the illusion of passing time. But one's self-consciousness exists only now, in the solipsism of the present moment.

Time and Matter

An obvious implication of solipsism of the present moment is that neither time nor matter exist. This is also a seldom mentioned feature of scientific realism. According to scientific realism, bodies exist in time, and time passes. A possible implication of this is that as time passes, bodies go out of existence in the previous, now non-existent, moment, and come into existence in the succeeding, now present moment. Bodies cannot exist at two moments at the same time. Thus the often stated scientific conclusion that the universe is 13.75 billion years old does not refer to a universe of material bodies that has been in existence for 13.75 billion years. It refers only to a material universe that exists at this moment. But the scientific fact about the age of the universe might be taken to imply falsely that bodies continue to exist in the past, in moments that no longer exist.

The scientific fact about the age of the universe also seems to imply that the bodies that exist now are the same bodies that existed in the past, as though bodies can travel through time. Perhaps they can, but a body can exist only at the present time. Bodies cannot exist spread over time, or at least one cannot perceive anything that is spread over time. One can perceive the existence of bodies only at the same time one perceives one's own existence—in the present moment. The age of the universe then—as are all other facts about the past—is implied from the universe as it exists only in the present moment.

One common-sensically and scientifically thinks of the universe, however, as an entity that persists through time, and thus that bodies persist in existence through time. On the other hand, one does not usually believe that bodies that exist now also exist in the future. But as the future is not yet, the past is no more. And as nothing now exists in the future, nothing now exists in the past.

It would seem that time might be an artifact of bodies. Suppose bodies are centers of force, or, even, that the entire material universe is a center of force. And this universal center of force is changing. Not changing all the time, just changing. Time is an artifact of this change. Time is not real, it just appears to be real as a result of the continuous changing of the material universe. One's memory recording this change is one's conscious response to this change. So there is no real time in the universe, just change, which one is conscious of in the form of memories, which memories exist in the present.

Shifting now to common-sense realism, one assumes that the bodies one perceives in the present moment are the same bodies one perceived in past moments. Never mind that past moments are gone. Common-sense bodies are assumed simply to travel through time, from one moment to the next. This gives rise to the notion of time travel popular in science fiction. The British philosopher Peter Geach was an avid reader of science fiction, and he particularly loved time-travel stories, so he could analyze the logical flaws in the time-travel gimmicks. I used to read science fiction too (most of it has gone to illogical fantasy these days, unreadable to a philosopher with my background) and Peter always thanked me profusely whenever I sent him a time-travel story he had not yet read.

On the web, there are a number of discussions in defense of the unreality of time. None of them have any relevance to the present discussion. Einstein's notion of the relativity of time to position in the universe is sometimes taken to imply that time is unreal, but on the contrary it is not an argument against the existence of time in the universe, but just an explication of an aspect of temporal perception of time in the universe.

Moments of time exist only momentarily and they do not stay in existence after their momentary appearance. Thus time is not a flow, it is not a river, it is a sequence of moments that succeed one another in existence, as Hume said, virtually instantaneously. Thus the blackboard representation of the stream of time as a line is quite misleading. I used to teach David Hume's view of the existence and passage of time by drawing that line with chalk in one hand, and erasing it immediately as I walked along the blackboard with an eraser in the other hand. Often some student would indignantly explain to me that this exercise does not make the point at all.

Both moments of time and the bodies that exist in those moments of time have only momentary existence—which, of course, logically follows. Nothing exists in the past, the past is gone. Nothing exists in the future, the future is not yet. The persisting universes of both common-sense realism and scientific realism, with their sea of time through which material bodies travel, do not exist. They are illogical artifacts.

So all right, one might say: logic be-damned. Of course the bodies one perceives at the present moment are the same as the bodies that existed in past moments. Never mind that to maintain this involves using one logical result to oppose a contrary logical result: such logic chopping is common in philosophy. And common-sense, at least, unlike science, does not require adhering strictly to logic. Why not simply declare, proclaim that bodies persist through time? One has the same body now one had in past moments, that is, assuming that there were any past moments. One can only proclaim—not experience or demonstrate that there were past moments, which is nothing one has any direct or certain evidence for, neither on common-sense nor on scientific ground. What has continuously amazed me as I have been working on this study (for many years as my memory-sense of time goes, as a matter of fact) is how many Anglo-American philosophers blithely go on asserting that bodies existed in the past, and that there was a past, even when they exhibit their comprehension of the empirical facts that lead to the conclusion that there is no way whatsoever to know that anything existed in the past, or to know that there was a past at all. Let me remind you again, that, like G. E. Moore, I insist that one is certain of lots of things. For example, I hold up my hand and say, "This is a hand." I am certain of it.

But I am not certain that my hand exists as a material object, or that it existed in the past, and philosophy, like science, does require strict adherence to logic. That is why I have undertaken this study of solipsism of the present moment—over the perceived period of many years. It is the result of strict adherence both to logic and to what one is certain of in one's conscious experience. It is clear that one can be certain only of the consciousness one has at the present moment, and only at the present moment.

On the grounds of both logic and conscious experience, then, one's self and the universe exist only in the present moment. This is very much opposed to the common-sense view of the universe one uncritically and unattentively assumes most of the time. It is also opposed to at least the way many scientists talk most of the time. What appears to be the case as time seems to pass is that one world of bodies goes out of existence and another world of bodies comes into existence instantaneously, moment after moment. This is what *seems* to happen. One does not notice the transition because one is always perceiving in the present moment. But on close analysis, it is clear that one perceives only one moment. Not one moment at a time. Just one moment. That moment is the only time there is. As remarked several times herein, the impression one has in the present moment that there has existed a sequence of past moments is an artifact or illusion of memory impressions in the present moment. One's world of sense-data, of impressions and ideas, exists only in the present moment. The world of actuality, the world that one perceives with certainty at the present moment, is the only world one can be assured exists. That is the simple point I persist in working to put across. It is what the solipsist knows for certain. The solipsist is not a skeptic. The solipsist is a realist who has a large body of certain knowledge about what he perceives at the present moment.

It will be the last moment one perceives before one dies.

Mind and Consciousness: The Hard Problem

Over the years I have accumulated and studied more than seventy-five books on or related to the subjects of mind and consciousness. It is a representative collection of how the subject has been treated in Anglo-American philosophy during the last fifty years. I have now gone through them to discover that "solipsism" appears in the indexes of only about a dozen of them. Most of these are just passages to identify solipsism, or to make a comment like the following by R. J. Hirst in his *The Problems of Perception*:

> In fact, of course, no one believes solipsism is satisfactory [what would it mean for solipsism to be "satisfactory"?], and philosophers would not give it moment's thought were it not for the difficulty of conclusively refuting it as opposed to showing that it is not plausible. (p. 162)

Hirst himself does not give solipsism more than a moment's thought, that is, he makes no attempt to refute it. He simply assumes that everyone will agree that it is not plausible. At least he recognizes that there are grounds for the position. Most philosophers—like Carnap and Goodman who construct systems out of private sense-data that imply solipsism—simply assume that no one will take solipsism seriously. I argue in the chapters on Carnap and Goodman above that it is a scandal that they get away with this. But it is not surprising given that the general response to solipsism in the philosophical literature is to ignore it or treat it without argument as being absurd.

When solipsism is discussed at any length, it is virtually always with a caveat to show that it is not taken seriously. For example, in his *The Intentional Stance*, Daniel C. Dennett utilizes what he calls

> methodological solipsism or psychology in the narrow sense . . . so narrowing our gaze as to lose sight of all the normal relations between things in the environment and

120

the activities within the system. . . . Our methodological
solipsism dictates that we ignore the environment in which
the organism resides—or has resided—but we can still
locate a boundary between the organism and its environment and determine the input and output surfaces of its
nervous system. (p. 141)

This is a typical example of what can only be called "pretend solipsism" that is purveyed in the literature to show that solipsism fails
because it does not account for what we common-sensically know
about the world and our senses. As I examine in the chapter on
Santayana, Santayana undertakes the only serious and detailed
attempt to refute solipsism in the literature—and admits failure.

Solipsism is recognized as a serious problem in a recent highly
influential book in the field of consciousness studies by David J.
Chalmers: *The Conscious Mind: In Search of a Fundamental Theory*
(1996). In this book, Chalmers introduces what he designates as
"The Hard Problem" of self-consciousness as follows:

The hardest part of the mind-body problem is the question:
how can a physical system give rise to conscious experience? Why and how [are] psychological properties . . .
accompanied by phenomenological properties . . . in
experience? What remains ill understood is the link
between the psychological mind and the phenomenological
mind. (p. 25)

This problem arises because

It is a fact about the human mind that whenever a phenomenological property is instantiated, a corresponding [con-
scious] psychological property is instantiated. Conscious
experience . . . is always tied to cognitive processing. . . .
(p. 22) [Then because] conscious experience does not supervene logically on the physical, and therefore cannot be
reductively explained (p. 71) . . . [n]o explanation given
wholly in physical terms can ever account for the emer-
gence of conscious experience. (p. 93) There is no *a priori*
entailment from physical facts to phenomenological facts.

. . . [T]here is no *a posteriori* necessary connection
between physical facts and phenomenological facts. (p. 94)
. . . *[T]here is an explanatory gap between the physical
level and conscious experience* [my italics] (p. 107) . . .
given that the laws of physics are ultimately cast in terms of
structure and dynamics. . . . The existence of (p. 121)
consciousness will always be a further fact relative to structural and dynamic facts, and so will be unexplained by a
physical account. . . . [W]e need only give up on a *reduc-
tive* explanation. The possibility of explaining consciousness nonreductively remains open. (122)

I give these lengthy quotations because although it may appear that
"the hard problem" can be simply stated in the short remark that
consciousness cannot be explained in physical terms, Chalmers
works hard to argue that the possibility of explaining conscious experience in physical terms remains open, although he himself never
gives any indication of how this might be accomplished. That is, he
says that "it remains plausible that consciousness supervenes *naturally* on the physical," although he gives no description of how, and the
only boost he gives the possibility is stressing the word "naturally."
He says that the dualism implied here is not a substance dualism such
as Descartes's, but instead

a kind of *property* dualism: conscious experience involves
properties of an individual that are not implied by the
physical properties of that individual, although they may
depend lawfully on those properties. Consciousness is a
feature Of the world over and above the physical features
of the world. This is not to say it is a separate
"substance". . . . All we know is that there are properties of individuals in this world—the phenomenal properties—that are ontologically independent of physical
properties. . . . It remains plausible . . . that consciousness *arises* from a physical basis, even though it is not
entailed by that basis. (125)

Again, I give these lengthy quotations to show that Chalmers does understand the problem of solipsism and how it arises. But what is the difference between implying and depending lawfully? Or between arising and entailing? Chalmers goes on to propose

> *psychophysical* laws, specifying how phenomenal (or protophenomenal properties depend on physical properties). These laws will not interfere with physical laws [which] already form a closed system. Instead, they will be *supervenience* laws, telling us how experience arises from physical processes. . . . (127)

I present all this because it shows how far removed Chalmers is from any coherent or satisfactory explanation of how consciousness *could* supervene on the physical (or even how we could know if it did). He admits this by saying at the end of his attempt to convince the reader that it might somehow be the case:

> Of course, at this stage we have very little idea what the relevant fundamental theory will look like. (127)

Chalmers does, however, come to a position. He sets out

The Logical Geography of the Issues

The argument for my view is an inference from four premises:

> 1. Conscious experience exists.
> 2. [It] is not logically supervenient on the physical.
> 3. If there are phenomena that are not logically supervenient on the physical facts, then materialism is false.
> 4. The physical domain is causally closed.

> Premises (1), (2), and (3) clearly imply the falsity of materialism. (161)

Chalmers presents his view as *Naturalistic Dualism*:

> Consciousness supervenes naturally on the physical, without supervening logically or "metaphysically." (162)

My exposition here of Chalmers's position in which he attempts to support the existence of conscious experience independent of the physical world is tedious, but no more so than his attempt to find a place for self-conscious minds with free will in the deterministic material world as we (common-sensically) know it.

I have quoted above virtually all Chalmers says in *The Conscious Mind* that is relative to solipsism, and, as I point out, he is conscious that he has no adequate refutation of the position. In his later book, *The Character of Consciousness* (2010), in 596 pages he does not even bring up the subject of solipsism, although he has an opening to do so in discussing

> The Double-Aspect Theory of Information . . . that information (or at least some information) has two basic aspects . . . a physical and a phenomenal. . . . (p. 26)

This leads him to remark, "An obvious question is whether *all* information has a phenomenal aspect." (p. 27) This question provides an obvious lead into a discussion of solipsism by way of the Absolute of Idealism, but Chalmers does not take it.

The only detailed attempt, or, I should say, claim, to refute solipsism that I know of in the contemporary literature is in *Dream, Death, and the Self* by J. J. Valberg (2007). Valberg takes solipsism to have been shown to be impossible by Wittgenstein. The argument, or position, is that:

> I am with others (others are with me) . . . other human beings . . . other *subjects*. . . . I regard other human beings as each at the center of a [consciousness] horizon that is coordinate with my horizon. I regard other human beings, all of us, as metaphysical equals. . . . [T]he Other's horizon is coordinate with my horizon . . . and so on. (p. 128)

Valberg takes the reader to be familiar with, and in agreement, with Wittgenstein's position that language implies, and thus proves, the existence of "Others," that is, multiple language users including oneself.

> The thought that I might be alone, that my MIND is the only mind, is in a real sense unthinkable. . . . When I reflect on my situation as an insider of our system of language games, as a thinker, the situation in which I find

myself with Others: the existence of other MINDS is already settled. . . . [W]hen the personal horizon dominates, other MINDS are included within mine. . . . To withdraw into the first person is, in effect, to withdraw into solipsism. (pp. 147–48)

Valberg takes Wittgenstein as Gospel. I understand Wittgenstein's arguments about language use, but see no grounds for the ontological claims Valberg makes on their basis. He engages in language-game play:

The solipsist (the solipsist in each of us) wants to say that my horizon is "the" horizon in the sense that it is *alone*. Aloneness is the essence of solipsism . . . my horizon includes all others. . . . We are all solipsists. (p. 187)

The world is *my* world: this is manifest in the fact that the limits of *language* (of that language which I alone understand) mean the limits of *my* world. (p. 198)

I believe the world, the same world that is present from within my horizon, is present from within your horizon, from within all horizons. (p. 201)

It seems clear that Valberg's declarations of faith in the existence of other minds do not constitute a refutation of solipsism.

Conclusion

There is only one theory of the universe as one experiences and knows it that is based on absolutely certain knowledge. All that one has immediate, certain knowledge of are the sensations and ideas one is conscious of in the present moment. And one knows with absolute certainty that one exists with the awareness of all that experience now in the present moment.

That the ordinary objects of naïve realism and the theoretical objects of scientific realism exist is not, and cannot ever be, known for certain. This does not bother most people, and most philosophers think the quest for certainty is misguided and absurd. But certainty is available, and the amount of certain knowledge one can have in the present moment is immense. It is enough to ground a lifetime.

Afterword

Solipsism—the thesis that one can be conscious only of one's own sensations and ideas in the present moment—is irrefutable. Suppose, then, that solipsism is true. So what? Would anything change in one's common-sense experience of the world? No, the world and everything in it would appear to one just as it always has. Nothing would change in one's scientific understanding of how the world works. All the laws of physics and biology, all the ways of understanding, and manipulating the world, would remain the same.

What about self-conscious beings other than oneself? They appear to exist, but if they do exist, there is no way to determine whether or not they have conscious experiences as one does. One cannot experience the experiences of other self-conscious beings, if there are any. If one did experience such experiences, those experiences would be one's own experiences, not the experiences of another. Even if there were a multitude of self-conscious perceivers in the universe, each of them would and could perceive only his or her own perceptions: sensations and ideas. It would make no difference to the being of a solipsist whether the world was populated with only one, or with many, solipsistic beings. There is no way any solipsistic being could determine whether or not there is only one, or many, solipsists.

In other words, to the question often proposed to the solipsist— "What about me? Are you claiming that I am not self-conscious?"— the response of the solipsist is that he or she has no way of knowing whether or not there are self-conscious beings in the universe other than himself or herself. Given that there is no reason to suppose that there is only one self-conscious being (oneself) in the universe, there is no reason to deny the possibility that there are more than one self-conscious being in the universe. One's solipsism would simply consist of one not having any direct awareness of, nor any other way to determine whether or not, any self-conscious beings exist other than oneself.

Just as there is no way to determine whether or not there are any self-conscious beings other than oneself in the world, there is no way to determine whether or not there is even a world other than the immediate conscious experiences one is having at the present moment.

My question is: So what?

Does it make any difference whether there are any self-conscious beings in the universe other than oneself? Other self-conscious beings who, like oneself, are confined to consciousness only of their own sensations and ideas?

Moreover, does it make any difference whether or not there is a material world outside the sensory experiences that one common-sensically takes to be caused by material things?

In his essay "The Will to Believe," the father of American pragmatism, William James, provided an answer to a similar question that plagues human beings: Does God exist? James points out that the question cannot be answered by appeal to any empirical test. Consequently, James concludes, you can choose whichever you want: God exists, or God does not exist. Later, James remarked that the essay should have been titled "The Right to Believe," not "The Will to Believe." Because there is no way to determine either by reason or by sensory experience whether or not God exists, one can believe whichever one wants. Similarly, because there is no way to determine either by reason or by sensory experience whether or not other self-conscious beings than oneself exists, one can believe whichever one wants.

James concludes that if one believes God exists, one will act differently from the way one would act if one does not believe God exists. Is the case similar with solipsism? If a solipsist believes that he or she is the only conscious being in the universe, will he or she act differently from how he or she would act if he or she believed that there were other conscious persons (perhaps themselves solipsists confined to their own momentary experiences) in the universe? James would say that it depends on the person. It seems to me that a confirmed solipsist might very well forget that he or she is the only conscious person in the universe, and thus go about his or her life behaving just as though the universe were populated by other self-conscious people like oneself. Would it make any difference to one's experience? That probably would depend on whether the solipsist had a morbid or a cheerful sense of life, but the basic answer is no. A solipsist would go about his or her life—at least most of the time—as though the world were populated by lots of other self-conscious people.

After all, if solipsism were true, would anything in the solipsist's experience be different from what it would be if solipsism were false? No. So why worry about it?

I have shown how a number of philosophers have tried—and failed—to refute solipsism. This failure is taken to be a great flaw in empiricism, and at the same time a great danger in rationalism. The principles of empiricism are not adequate to refute solipsism. The principles of rationalism lead to solipsism.

That covers the waterfront of Western philosophy.

Solipsism is iron-clad irrefutable.

What is to be done?

On the other hand, why assume that if solipsism is true, there is anything to be done?

If one is a—the—solipsist, the only self-conscious entity in the universe, an entity that exists only at the present moment, with no way of knowing whether or not anything, including itself, ever existed at any past moment or will exist at any future moment—rather than asking what is to be done about it, why isn't the question: So what? What difference does it make whether or not one is the only existing conscious being? And what difference does it make whether one's being exists through time, or only in the present moment? As far as one's experience goes, it makes no difference at all.

Empirically, through examining one's experience, there is no way of telling whether one is the only existing self-conscious entity or not. Nor is there any way of telling whether or not one exists only in the present moment, or persists in existing through successive moments. Precisely: if one's experience would be the same whether one's consciousness exists only in the present moment, or persists through successive moments, if one cannot tell which is the case through examination of one's experiences, then what difference does it make?

According to the empirical meaning criterion, to have meaning a statement must make a difference in one's experience of the world depending on whether that statement is true or false. Thus it might seem reasonable to conclude that because the answer to the question of whether or not solipsism is true cannot be answered by reference to one's empirical experience, nor can the question of whether or not one's consciousness persists through time or exists only in the present moment be answered by reference to one's empirical experience—those questions make no intelligible sense.

But the thesis of solipsism is perfectly intelligible. There may be no possible way of disconfirming it, but on the other hand, one confirms one's existence in the present moment every moment of one's conscious being. One has no certain knowledge of the existence of anything else.

Finally, the question always arises: So what causes the experiences the solipsist has in the present moment? Cause? As Hume points, there is no ground in experience for postulating the notion of causation. Why does there need to be a cause? The solipsistic experience just is, in the present moment.

A major result in Western philosophy from insisting on causes is that it leads to the question of the ultimate cause, and the ultimate answer: God. God is the cause of everything. And God creates everything out of nothing. This is not a satisfactory answer, and of course it has made legions of logical positivists view the notion of God as contradictory nonsense.

But as David Hume would point out, the lack of causation in solipsism make it no worse off—even if its ultimate results are no better—than any other metaphysical system in Modern philosophy.

Appendix: You and Me, Babe!

Hi ya, babe!

Wait, don't go away.

Tell me, where were you when you picked up this book and started to read? I do not mean were you in the kitchen or the front room. I mean, where were *you*? When you started to read? Did you lose consciousness of your surroundings? Of yourself? Are you asking yourself what has this guy got in mind? What did *you* have in mind? What *do* you have in mind?

I had in mind this question: How many voices are in your head? Right now.

Let's see, there's my voice. Then there's your voice, answering my questions. So you have at least my voice and your voice.

Look, are you alone? I mean, there's nobody else talking to you, is there? If there is, we'd better try this some other time. What I have to say is rather intimate.

You're alone. All right, we can continue. You see, I want to know just how many voices you hear right now. When there are not any people around, when you're just sitting there, reading. You hear my voice, and you hear your own. Two voices. Is that all? Are there ever more than two? Is there ever only one? What about when you're not reading, when you're just thinking?

I'll tell you something. When I think, I talk to myself. Inside my head, of course. What about you? When you're thinking, do you carry on an interior dialogue? When you think, do you have a conversation with yourself? Two voices?

Is there ever only one voice? What would single-voiced thinking be like? Look, here's a story. A true story. It happened to my mother-in-law.

There's this little girl, see? She's larking around in a sunflower patch.

Suddenly, she stops. She looks at the sunflower in her hand. There are hundreds all about. But now, there is something else.

She thinks: "I am me."

The words come to her.

"I am me. This is a sunflower. It's not me. I'm not it. I am me. Elaine Lance! I am six years old, and I am me. Me! Me, me, me! And nobody else in the whole world is me but me!"

Marcel Proust had such an experience. Maybe one out of a dozen people do. Alas, I never did. Yet, here I am. And you, are you there?

Maybe single-voiced thinking would be like what the little girl did before she realized who she was. There was this voice babbling all the time. She just did not know it was *her* voice. She did not know *she* was thinking, is that it?

So whose voice did she think it was?

She did not think it was anybody's voice, because she did not yet know that voices were had, that there was her voice and other voices.

So perhaps before, the little girl thought with a single voice. But how could *she*? She did not even know it was her. She could not say to herself that it was herself because she had not yet noticed that she was herself.

She had conversations with her dolls. But she did not yet know that *they* were not *her*. So she was carrying on a conversation with herself, but just did not know it? Because you can't have a single-voiced conversation. Can you?

Yo!

I'm worried that you're forgetting me. When you read the last paragraph, was I there? I mean, was it me or you talking? I'm here, but I'm worried that you'll lose me.

Sometimes when you're reading, maybe you do not notice any talking in your head at all. Not that you were thinking of something else while you were reading, you were paying attention. There just were not any voices.

Was it like this? You're driving on a long automobile trip. All at once you're ten miles farther down the road. You think back and remember some scenery and passing a truck. But were *you* there at the time?

Or you're at the symphony. When it's over, you look up. Where are you? Then you remember the music.

The problem is: Where were you? Were *you* driving? Did *you* hear the music? Like somebody asking what time it is and you remember that a few minutes ago the clock struck three but you did not notice it at the time.

In these cases the inner dialogue was absent. If you *had* been there, would not each situation have been a sort of conversation? The highway and the music talking to you and you replying? Is not there always a conversation if you notice that it's *you* who's there?

When you reflect on your thinking, or pay attention to what *you* are doing, there are at least two voices. Reflexive, attentive thought is two-voiced because it involves self-awareness. It points back to the thinker as well as to its object.

Don't go away! I just had great anxiety that we lost contact in that last paragraph. Please stay with me.

(Of course that's pathetic. What if you say, "Not me, buddy," and quit reading. But who would you be talking to? Who is buddy?)

(I *like* you talking back. But you know perfectly well that I can't hear you. So who are you talking to?)

This is getting too intense. Let's relax for a minute. Do not go to sleep! Just relax.

It's nice like this, quiet, just sitting. I wonder, do you think we could be friends? Think about it. I mean, we're making a serious attempt to get together. No barriers, just you and me.

Quiet.

Relaxed.

I do find a comfort in it, just being with you. There's a directness about it, my writing, your reading. Me. You. It's very satisfying. Actually, I do not feel the need to say much to you now. I'm just content to be here with you, our being here together.

OK? Time to get back to work?

More questions. Were you cheating just now? I was. It was not just me and you. I was there with us. I was thinking how I could make you stay with me. I was talking to myself while I was there with you.

I'm often self-conscious like that. Aware that *I'm* thinking about something. And when I'm talking to you, there are three voices. Just now, one of them was going on to you, and two others were talking back and forth worrying whether I was keeping your attention.

Sometimes you're too self-conscious, when you're paying more attention to yourself than to what you're doing. You're apt to get embarrassed or pompous when that happens. It makes you awkward or ineffective. But that's not really me, you say.

If it's not really you, who is it? Audie Murphy stormed up a hill and took a German machine-gun nest single-handed. Afterward he said he did not remember a thing. And they gave *him* a medal?

If you set yourself on automatic pilot and come up with the answer to a problem without thinking about it, can you still get credit for the results? Surely you can't be praised or blamed for doing something unless at least you know you're doing it. Or are you sometimes like an oven that's programmed to go on to warm the casserole for supper? The oven does not know it's warming the casserole. You do not know you're solving the problem.

Unless you know what you're doing, how can *you* be said to be doing it? Can you blaspheme while you are asleep, mad, bewitched, drugged, hypnotized, drunk, coerced, or ignorant of theology?

Wait!

Look, suppose you've been praying, urging God to answer. Then this voice comes to you, in your head, and it says, "Quit whining."

"What?" you say. "Who are you?"

"Who else?" the voice says.

"But are you really God, talking to *me*?"

"Sure thing."

This stuns you. How can it be?

"How do I know you're really God?" you ask.

The voice heaves a celestial sigh. "I suppose you want a sign," the voice says. "Is not it enough that I'm talking to you?"

It is not enough. The voice refuses to pick the winning lottery ticket.

No one else can hear the voice. It begins to give orders.

"Go to Mass every morning. Say a thousand Hail Marys. Do not Take My Name in Vain."

It is very domineering.

One day it begins to make indecent suggestions. You say to yourself that this can't be right, and go to a priest. The priest thinks demonic possession is bull, and sends you to a psychiatrist. The psychiatrist says that you yourself are the source of the voice in your head. When the voice tells you to shoot the psychiatrist, he sends you in for electric shocks that get rid of it.

Of course, if the shocks kill *all* the voices in your head, *you* are dead, right?

What if the voice came out of the air?

"Hi," it says. "Call me God."

You look around, but nobody's there.

"Where are you?" you say.

"Everywhere and nowhere, really, but I suppose you could say that I'm right here in front of you, where my voice is coming from."

A friend comes into the room to see who you're talking to. Your friend does not hear the voice. Neither does your psychiatrist. After the electric shocks you do not hear it anymore, either.

You do hear inner voices, though, right?

How come they do not cart you off to the funny farm for carrying on this conversation with me? I'm a voice in your head, too. In fact, if you had ever heard me talking out loud, now when you read me, it might even be *as though* you hear me talking out loud. It's like that with authors whose distinctive speaking voices you've heard, is not it? When I read the wonderful writer, Stanley Elkin, I can not not hear his voice. And Stanley is dead as a doornail. But God! is he glad I can hear his voice.

They do not send you to the funny farm, because you're just reading. This voice is directed by me, but it's really yours. It's a well-known phenomenon. They even let God talk through a book. But that's just a manner of speaking, right?

It's really your voice. I mean, these voices are in *your* head. And if they're in your head, they're yours. Whose else could they be? Of course one of them is saying things you might not have thought of by yourself, but that's allowed when you're reading, right? It's my words, but your voice? Right? It does not bother you or your psychiatrist, because you have this text in front of you. When you're reading, there does not need to be anybody else.

Not so fast. *I'm* the author of this text. You'd better believe it, my voice is in your head, too. You can't ignore me.

135

"Why not?" you say. "You might be dead. Lots of authors are, you know, like Stanley. And *they're* not talking, ha, ha."

Very funny. Listen. What if I were to tell you that this was typed by a team of monkeys? You'd groan, right? It makes a difference, right? This author—me—is *not* dead. OK? (Actually, there may be a problem with this sentence after a few years.)

But what difference would it make if I were dead?

"Sigh. I hear you talking."

All right! Now tell me. Am I more important to you, or are you more important to me?

"Well, like they say, it takes two to tango."

Yo, babe! Now you got it. Shall we dance?

* * *

Yo, babe! You still here?

I thought so.

The conversation continues. Everything is the same. You and me. I'll always be here to talk to you. So solipsism is not quite as lonely as one might have thought. You see those crazy old ladies with all their belongings in a grocery cart, pushing it along, talking to themselves, stopping now and then to make a point. They're not crazy. They're just like you and me, talking to themselves all the time.

What's that you say? They're still crazy?

Nah.

Well, you're not very talkative today. I understand. But just remember, you never need be lonely. I'm always here, always ready for conversation.

Carry on!

* * *

P.S. So you hear voices in your head, particularly when you read to yourself. But what makes you think you hear voices anywhere else but in your head? Think about it. When someone is standing in front of you and talking to you, you hear that person's voice, right? But where do you hear it? You hear it in your head. You assume that the source of the voice is the person standing in front of you and talking to you, but how do you know that what is in front of you is a person, a conscious person, purposely talking to you by making noises you hear and understand? You have never had any direct acquaintance with that person. Or with any other person, as far as that goes, except yourself.

So it isn't odd that you have conversations with yourself. You don't know for sure of the existence of any other conscious person. Who else is there you can have a conversation with that you can be sure is a self-conscious person? Like you.

Bibliography

Armstrong, D. M. *A Materialist Theory of Mind.* London: Routledge& Kegan Paul, 1968.

———. *The Mind-Body Problem: An Opinionated Introduction.* Boulder: Westview Press, 1999.

Augustine, Saint. *Confessions.* Translated with an Introduction and Notes by Henry Chadwick. Oxford: Oxford University Press, 1991.

Austin, J. L. *Sense and Sensibilia.* Oxford: Oxford University Press, 1964

Ayer, Alfred Jules. *The Foundations of Empirical Knowledge.* London: Macmillan & Co., 1940.

———. *Language, Truth and Logic.* London: Victor Gollance, 1948.

———. "One's Knowledge of Other Minds." In *Philosophical Essays,* 191–214. London: Macmillan, 1954.

Bergmann, Gustav. *The Metaphysics of Logical Positivism.* New York: Longmans, Green and Co., 1954.

Berkeley, George. *A Treatise Concerning the Principles of Human Knowledge.* In Calkins, *op. cit.,* 124–216. First published in 1710.

———. *Three Dialogues between Hylas and Philonous.* La Salle: Open Court Publishing Company, 1955. First published in London in 1713.

Bermúdez, José Luis. *The Paradox of Self-Consciousness.* Cambridge: MIT Press, 2000.

Blackmore, Susan. *Conversations on Consciousness.* Oxford: Oxford University Press, 2007

Block, Ned, Owen Flanagan, and Güven Güzelder, eds. *The Nature of Consciousness.* Cambridge: MIT Press, 1997.

Borst, C. V. *The Mind/Brain Identity Theory*. New York: Macmillan, 1970.

Bowsma, O. K. "Descartes' Scepticism of the Senses." *Mind* 54 (1954): 313–22.

Bradley, F. H. *Appearance and Reality*. 2nd ed. London: Oxford University Press, 1897 [1st ed. 1893].

Broad, C. D. *The Mind and its Place in Nature*. London: Routledge and Kegan Paul, 1925.

Calkins, Mary W. Introduction to *Berkeley: Essay, Principles, Dialogues, with Selections from Other Works*, ix–lvi. New York: Charles Scribner's Sons, 1957.

Carnap, Rudolf. *The Logical Structure of the World: Pseudoproblems in Philosophy*. Berkley: University of California Press, 1967.

Castañeda, Héctor-Neri. "Private Language Problem." In *The Encyclopedia of Philosophy*, edited by Paul Edwards, 6:458–64. New York: Macmillan, 1967.

Chalmers, David J. *The Conscious Mind: In Search of a Fundamental Theory*. Oxford: Oxford University Press, 1996.

———. *The Character of Consciousness*. Oxford: Oxford University Press, 2010.

Churchland, Patricia Smith. *Neurophilosophy: Toward a Unified Science of the Mind*. Cambridge: MIT Press, 1986.

Churchland, Paul M. *Scientific Realism and the Plasticity of Mind*. Cambridge: Cambridge University Press, 1979.

Cummins, Robert. *Meaning and Mental Representation*. Cambridge: MIT Press, 1991.

Cunningham, G. Watts. *The Idealistic Argument in Recent British British and American Philosophy*. New York & London: The Century Company, 1933.

Clark, Andy. *Being There: Putting Brain, Body, and World Together Again*. Cambridge: MIT Press, 1997.

Cooney, Brian, ed. *The Place of Mind*. London: Wadsworth, 2000.

Cornman, James W. *Perception, Common Sense, and Science*. New Haven: Yale University Press, 1975.

Craver, Carl F. *Explaining the Brain: Mechanisms and the Mosaic Unity of Neuroscience*. Oxford: Clarendon Press, 2007.

Damasio, Antonio. *The Feeling of What Happens: Body and Emotion in the Making of Consciousness*. New York: Harcourt Brace & Co., 1999.

Dennett, Daniel C. *Content and Consciousness: An Analysis of Mental Phenomena*. London: Routledge & Kegan Paul, 1969.

———. *The Intentional Stance*. Cambridge: MIT Press, 1990.

———. *Consciousness Explained*. Boston: Little Brown and Co., 1991.

Descartes, René. *Discourse on the Method* (1637). In *The Philosophical Writings of Descartes*, vol. I, translated by John Cottingham et al., 111–51. Cambridge: Cambridge University Press, 1985.

Descartes, René. *Meditations on First Philosophy* (1641). In *The Philosophical Writings of Descartes*, vol. II, translated by John Cottingham et al., 1–62. Cambridge: Cambridge University Press, 1984.

Descombes, Vincent. *The Mind's Provisions: A Critique of Cognitivism*. Princeton: Princeton University Press, 2001.

Ewing, A. C., ed. *The Idealist Tradition from Berkeley to Blanchard*. Glencoe: The Free Press, 1957.

Feigl, Herbert. *The "Mental" and the "Physical": The Essay and a Postscript*. Minneapolis: University of Minnesota Press, 1958.

Fichte, Johann Gottlieb. *Science of Knowledge*. Translated by Peter Heath & John Lachs. Cambridge: Cambridge University Press, 1982.

Flanagan, Owen. *Consciousness Reconsidered*. Cambridge: MIT Press, 1992.

———. *The Really Hard Problem: Meaning in a Material World*. Cambridge: MIT Press, 2007.

Fodor, Jerry A. *The Modularity of Mind*. Cambridge: MIT Press, 1983.

———. *The Language of Thought*. Cambridge: Harvard University Press, 1975.

Goodman, Nelson. *The Structure of Appearance.* 2nd ed. New York: Bobbs-Merrill, 1966.

Hannan, Barbara. *Subjectivity & Reduction: An Introduction to the Mind-Body Problem.* Boulder: Westview Press, 1994.

Hare, John Casper. *On Myself, and Other, Less Important Subjects.* Princeton: Princeton University Press, 2009.

Hartshorne, Charles. *The Logic of Perfection.* La Salle: Open Court Publishing Company, 1962.

Hirst, R. J. *The Problems of Perception.* London: George Allen and Unwin, 1959.

Honderich, Ted. *On Consciousness.* Pittsburgh: University of Pittsburgh Press, 2004.

Hume, David. *A Treatise of Human Nature.* Oxford: The Clarendon Press, 1955. First published in 1739.

———. *Dialogues Concerning Natural Religion.* Edited by Richard H. Popkin. Indianapolis: Hackett Publishing Company, 1980. First published in 1779.

James, William. "Is Radical Empiricism Solipsistic?" *The Journal of Philosophy, Psychology and Scientific Methods* 2 (1905): 235–38.

———. *The Principles of Psychology.* Bristol: Thoemmes Press, 1890.

———. "The Will to Believe." In *Essays in Pragmatism,* 88–109. New York: Hafner, 1948. First published in 1896.

Joad, C. E. M., C. A. Richardson, and F. C. S. Schiller. "Symposium: Is Neo-Idealism Reducible to Solipsism?" *Proceedings of the Aristotelian Society. Supplementary Volumes.* Vol. 3 (1923): 129–47.

Kant, Immanuel. *Critique of Pure Reason.* 2nd ed. Translated by Norman Kemp Smith. London: Macmillan, 1956.

———. *Prolegomena to Any Future Metaphysics That Will Be Able to Come Forward as Science.* Revised ed. Translated by Gary Hatfield. Cambridge: Cambridge University Press, 2004 [1st ed. 1997].

Kripke, Saul. *Wittgenstein on Rules and Private Language*. Oxford: Basil Blackwell, 1982.

Lycan, William G. *Consciousness*. Cambridge: MIT Press, 1987.

———. *Consciousness and Experience*. Cambridge: MIT Press, 1996.

Lycan, William G. and Jesse Prinz, eds. *Mind and Cognition: An Anthology*. Oxford: Basil Blackwell, 2008.

Mach, Ernst. *The Analysis of Sensations and the Relation of the Physical to the Psychical*. 5th ed. New York: Dover, 1959.

Malebrache, Nicolas. *The Search After Truth*. Translated by Thomas M. Lennon and Paul J. Olscamp. Columbus: Ohio State University Press, 1980. First published 1674–75.

Matthews, Gareth B. "Descartes and the Problem of Other Minds." In *Essays on Descartes' Meditations*, edited by Amélie Oksenberg Rorty, 141–52. Berkeley: University of California Press, 1986.

———. *Thought's Ego in Augustine and Descartes*. Ithaca: Cornell University Press, 1992.

McGinn, Colin. *The Problem of Consciousness*. Oxford: Blackwell, 1991.

———. *The Mysterious Flame: Minds in a Material World*. Oxford: Basil Blackwell, 1999.

McTaggart, John McTaggart Ellis. *The Nature of Existence*. 2 vols. Edited by C. D. Broad. Cambridge: Cambridge University Press, 1921–1927.

Metzinger, Thomas. *Being No One: The Self-Model Theory of Subjectivity*. Cambridge: MIT Press, 2003.

Moore, G. E. "Proof of an External World." In *Philosophical Papers*, 127–50. London: George Allen & Unwin, 1932.

Nagel, Thomas. *Mind and Cosmos: Why the Materialist Neo-Darwinian Conception of Nature Is Almost Certainly False*. Oxford: Oxford University Press, 2012.

Parfit, Derek. "Personal Identity." *The Philosophical Review* 80 (1971): 3–27.

———. *Reasons and Persons*. Oxford: Oxford University Press, 1984.

Perry, J. *Possibility and Consciousness*. Cambridge: MIT Press, 2001.

Perry, Ralph Barton. "The Ego-Centric Predicament." *Journal of Philosophy, Psychology, and Scientific Methods* 7 (1910): 5–14.

Popkin, Richard H. *The History of Skepticism From Savonarola to Bayle*. Oxford: Oxford University Press, 2003.

Popper, Karl R. & John C. Eccles. *The Self and Its Brain: An Argument for Interactionism*. New York: Springer-International, 1977.

Rhees, Rush. "Wittgenstein's Notes for Lectures on 'Private Experience' and 'Sense Data.'" *The Philosophical Review* 77 (1968): 271–75.

Rollins, C. D. "Solipsism." In *The Encyclopedia of Philosophy*, edited by Paul Edwards, 7:487–91. New York: Macmillan and The Free Press, 1967.

Royce, Josiah. *The World and the Individual, Gifford Lectures, Second Series. Nature, Man, and the Moral Order*. New York: Macmillan, 1901.

———. *Lectures on Modern Idealism*. New Haven: Yale University Press, 1919.

Russell, Bertrand. *The Problems of Philosophy*. London: Oxford University Press, 1951. First published in 1910.

———. *An Outline of Philosophy*. London: George Allen & Unwin, 1927.

———. *A History of Western Philosophy*. New York: Simon and Schuster, 1945.

———. *Human Knowledge: Its Scope and Limits*. London: George Allen & Unwin, 1948.

———. *The Autobiography of Bertrand Russell*. Vol. 2, *1914–1944*. Boston: Little, Brown, 1968.

Ryle, Gilbert. *The Concept of Mind*. London: Hutchinson, 1949.

Santayana, George. *Skepticism and Animal Faith: Introduction to a*

System of Philosophy. Dover Publications, 1955. First published in 1923.

Schiller, F. C. S. "Is Absolute Idealism Solipsistic?" *The Journal of Philosophy, Psychology, and Scientific Methods* 3, no. 4 (1906): 85–89.

———. "Solipsism." *Mind* 18 (1909, New Series): 169–83.

Searle, John. *Minds, Brains and Science*. Cambridge: Harvard University Press, 1984.

———. *The Rediscovery of the Mind*. Cambridge: MIT Press, 1992.

———. *The Mystery of Consciousness*. New York: NYREV, 1997.

Snow, D. E. *Schelling and the End of Idealism*. Albany: State University of New York Press, 1996.

Soames, Scott. *Philosophical Analysis in the Twentieth Century*. 2 vols. Princeton: Princeton University Press, 2003.

Spiegelberg, Herbert. "On the I-Am-Me Experience in Childhood and Adolescence." In *Steppingstones Toward and Ethics for Fellow Existers: Essays 1955–1983*, 29–48. Dordrecht: Martinus Nijoff, 1986.

Sprigge, T. L. S. *The Vindication of Absolute Idealism*. Edinburgh: Edinburgh University Press, 1983.

———. *James and Bradley: American Truth and British Reality*. Chicago & La Salle: Open Court, 1993.

Stebbing, L. Susan. *Logical Positivism and Analysis*. London: H. Milford, 1933.

Todd, William. *Analytical Solipsism*. The Hague: Martinus Nijhoff, 1968.

Tolle, Eckhart. *The Power of Now*. New York: New World Library, 1999.

Valberg, J. J. *Dream, Death, and the Self*. Princeton: Princeton University Press, 2007.

Watson, Richard A. *The Philosopher's Joke: Essays in Form and Content*. Buffalo: Prometheus Books, 1990.

———. *The Breakdown of Cartesian Metaphysics*. Indianapolis: Hackett, 1998.

————. *Cogito Ergo Sum: The Life of René Descartes*. Revised 2nd ed. Boston: David R. Godine, 2007.

Wegner, Daniel M. *The Illusion of Conscious Will*. Cambridge: MIT Press, 2002.

Wisdom, John. *Other Minds*. Oxford: Oxford University Press, 1953.

Wittgenstein, Ludwig. *Tractatus Logico-philosophicus*. London: Routledge & Kegan Paul, 1922.

————. *Philosophical Investigations*. Oxford: Basil Blackwell, 1953.

————. *On Certainty*. Edited by G. E. M. Anscombe and G. H. von Wright. Oxford: Basil Blackwell, 1969.